THE MAN WITH THREE FINGERS

Other books by the same author :

THE MAN WITH THREE FINGERS

J. B. Donovan

SCRIPTURE UNION 5 Wigmore Street, London W1H 0AD

ISBN 0 85421 386 4

Photoset and printed in Malta by St. Paul's Press Limited

CONTENTS

OPERATION ANDES

WITH a night-splitting roar the small red plane taxied along the gravel runway and rose abruptly over the blackness of the Bolivian forest, heading south-west.

The two Englishmen slithered to a halt. The slighter of the two turned to run for a second plane, but the other gripped his arm.

"No need, Keith—he's saved us the trouble! That was the fuel supply plane he took—and its own tanks are nearly empty. He hasn't enough for more than fifty miles."

"And there's nothing but solid forest and mountain for at least five hundred." Keith Oban spoke the thought in both minds.

Dan Brent nodded. "All we can do is wait for the smash, then go and pick up the pieces. Not that there'll be any pieces with that load," he added grimly.

They watched the dark outline of the plane against the stars until it merged with the black ridge of the Andes forty miles away. Fifteen taut minutes, then—like the spurt of a match in a dark room—the explosion.

Keith Oban's lean face tightened for a moment, but he showed no other sign. Dan Brent let out a long, slow breath. . . .

*   *   *   *

Three days later, in an austere, safe-like office of the Counter Espionage Division, Special Branch, in London, a bulky dossier was removed from a filing cabinet and locked away. A confidential secretary typed out an index card: "Matthew Gregory. Deceased. File closed". The card was dated, and filed.

And in every government in Europe at least one man breathed a private sigh of relief, and went about his work with an unfamiliar sense of freedom. The man with three fingers would do no more harm to anyone.

1

DEAD MAN'S HAND

"Good old Hyde Park!"

Mike Brent leaned out of the taxi window and took a hearty sniff of stifling July air. "Never feel I'm back in London till I see Hyde Park." He flapped his damp shirt and pushed thick sandy hair off his sunburnt forehead. "Phew, it's hot! Don't know how you keep cool G.B.!"

His companion turned a neat dark head from the other window and smiled. Like everything else about Geff Brooke his smile was clear-cut and controlled.

"Probably because I can sit still for two minutes on end, my son: which you haven't done once in the six months I've known you!"

Mike snorted cheerfully, and spread himself on the taxi seat. "Anyway—no more old bones for twelve weeks. They're a bit much in this sort of weather. Phew! Who'd be a medical student!"

"You were briefing me about your uncle," said G.B.

"Sounds queer to call him my uncle. He's not a great deal older than us—only thirty or so."

"Not a great deal," said G.B. dryly.

Mike waved clammy hands. "Well, what's twelve years or so? Anyway—I've always called him Dan. He's my legal guardian as well—did I get that far?"

"You were telling me about his work with Counter Espionage," said G.B. patiently.

Mike snapped his fingers. "That's right. I was telling you about the bloke they called the Man with Three

3

Fingers: apparently the little finger of his left hand was missing. It seems he was something out of the top drawer in espionage. Didn't work for any particular country, but apparently he had a genius for ferreting out things that governments didn't want other governments to know. Then he'd contact the government he knew would give him the most cash for the information.''

"That kind of spy doesn't usually amount to much, does he?"

"Not usually. I don't know all the ins and outs, but it seems this one was a really clever sort. Strong enough to call his own tune every time."

"And Dan was put on to him?"

"Yes. He and Keith—a pal of his in the same game, you remember—tracked him for months. Cornered him at last somewhere in the wilds of South America, and he blew himself up in a plane. They never could decide whether or not he did it on purpose. They searched the area for days, but didn't find so much as a toenail. Plane wasn't much better." Mike gazed out of the window, his cheerful face screwed up in a puzzled frown. "How a couple of toughs like that can go back to digging up old ruins and ferreting out ancient tribes beats me. Incidentally, G.B., Dan'll be interested that you picked up that Quechua dialect so quickly!"

"I'm a good pupil!" G.B. smiled.

"I'm a good teacher, you mean!"

The taxi drew up in Exhibition Road, Kensington.

"Museum of Anthropology & Ethnology, gents!" announced the driver, and deposited two weighty holdalls on the dusty pavement.

Mike tactfully studied the depressing grey columns of the façade, while G.B. paid the driver. He would have been content, of necessity, with a plain bus if it had been left to him.

They lugged the bags up the steps and dumped them on the polished floor of the entrance hall.

"Well, if it isn't Mr. Brent!" A perspiring commission-aire rolled forward to greet them. "'Ave a good journey down, sir? Mr. Brent's up in 'is office if you'd like to go straight up!" He turned round, waving a lordly arm and puffing out a shaggy black moustache. "Jackson! Jackson —ah, there 'e is! New 'ere, sir," he muttered to Mike. "Not always as quick off the mark as you'd like. But 'e copped it pretty bad in the War, sir, so we—ah, Jackson, take the gents' bags, hif you please. This 'ere is Mr. Michael Brent—nephew of *our* Mr. Brent."

Jackson limped out of the dimness of the passage—and Mike's inside nearly turned over. He wasn't an elderly man, just tinged with grey, and his left side seemed to be almost paralysed; but Mike was conscious of nothing but his eye. A vivid, discoloured scar ran from his forehead to his cheek, with the most disconcerting result Mike had ever seen.

Mike pulled himself together. "Er, how do you do, Mr. Jackson. We'll—er—call for the bags on our way out later."

"I suppose I ought to have welcomed him to the fold or something," he muttered as they went up the broad stair-case; "but that eye put me properly off my stroke. You'd think he'd wear a patch or something, wouldn't you! Looked as though he'd been pretty badly damaged. What d'you think it was—bayonet?"

G.B. nodded absently, his interested dark eyes taking in the cases in the long light gallery. "Possibly. What does Dan do exactly?" he went on.

"He and Keith still work together, Keith organizes all the field excavations and so on, while Dan cleans and patches up the finds, and studies them. He's working on some crates of Inca stuff now. That's their speciality."

"Have they found anything really interesting? You said something in the taxi about ancient tribes."

"That's right. Some of them go back for centuries with-out any change. But it seems that most tribes either go on developing—you know, arts and crafts and civilization, and so on—or else they come to a peak, and then start to degenerate. We do know that some who were quite civilized three or four hundred years ago—like the Incas—have gone right back to quite primitive ways."

"Well, the Spaniards were responsible for that, I suppose."

"You mean Pizarro and Co.? Yes, I suppose so, more or less. Stripped them of everything worth having and treated them rough generally. Wonder any survived at all. Queer, isn't it," he mused: "refugees aren't as modern as you'd think, are they! I suppose it was just the same for the Incas, trying to find somewhere the Spaniards couldn't get at them, as it is for some of the middle Europeans and Middle Eastern people now."

G.B. stopped by a showcase. "That's Inca work, isn't it?" He indicated a small snake, beautifully moulded in gold. "They were pretty clever, weren't they?"

Mike agreed. "Rich, too. That's what the Conquistadores—and the Elizabethans—were after, of course."

G.B. nodded towards a saucer-shaped dish. "Is that Inca as well?"

"Yes: it came from Machu Picchu. Those squares and triangles on it are typical. And that thing like a cork with red and blue feathers stuck in it is an earplug. Cheerful lot, I gather: keen on colours and feathers and things. And music, even."

G.B. studied the dish more closely. "Machu Picchu—that was the famous 'lost city'?"

"That's right. The Incas kept it dark from the Spaniards, and the local Indians wouldn't talk about it afterwards—until Professor Bingham discovered it in—er—1911, I think it was."

"Intriguing," G.B. mused as they moved on down the gallery. "A city of that size—well, big enough by their standards—absolutely lost to the rest of the world for over three hundred years."

Mike nodded thoughtfully. "Some parts of the Andes are pretty difficult to get at—you know, with forests and so on. You could walk from here to John o' Groats and still be in the same forest."

They turned into a corridor, and Mike knocked at the last of the row of museum offices. There was no reply so they walked in.

"This is Dan's office. Probably in the lab." Mike twisted the handle of the inner door, and frowned. "That'd odd. He never locks the lab. door."

Another door on the right opened into a large room stuffed almost to the ceiling with packing cases, crates, webbing and loaded shelves. There was no sign of Dan, but Mike knew what to do. He stood in the doorway and shouted.

"Dan!"

There was a movement in the far left corner, and a khaki-overalled arm hooked itself over a crate. A rough weatherbeaten fair head sprinkled with shavings followed.

"Mike!" Dan Brent vaulted the crate and wrung Mike's hand, his face creasing in a wide smile of welcome. "And this is G.B.! Well, well!" He slapped Mike on the back. "There's someone else here I want you to see, too, Mike!" He led the way back to the office carrying a large earthenware bowl. "Come on into the lab."

He fitted the key.

"Isn't it a bit unusual to lock it?" Mike queried.

Dan's beaming face grew suddenly grave. "Unusual circumstances."

As Dan pushed open the door an African of the largest make loomed into Mike's field of vision.

"John Akobe!" Mike pumped the enormous hand with delight. "John Mwolu Akobe—how are you? It must be five years since I saw you last! What are you doing so far from Peru!"

"I am very well, thank you, young Mike." The deep

voice was still as unexpectedly soft, and the grip as powerful, as Mike remembered it—and the smile as broad. "I
came with—a consignment from Keith."

The slight hesitation didn't escape Mike. He looked at
Dan and grinned.

"Out with it, Dan: what's going on? John Akobe comes
all the way from Peru, apparently on his own, and you lock
him in the lab. Then when I ask why he has come he
doesn't know how much to tell me! Come on, now—
what've you got here? Has Keith unearthed the lost
treasure of the Incas or something?"

Dan placed the bowl on the bench. Then to Mike's
surprise he locked the outer office and store-room doors,
leaving the laboratory door wide open. He glanced at
them curiously.

"Strangely enough, you're not as far wrong as you
might think."

Dan brought out a cash box from the safe, and placed it
on the bench. "Tell me what you make of this."

He took out of the box what appeared to be an irregular lump of rock crystal, the size of a hen's egg.
He laid it on the palm of his hand in the path of the sun.
"Take a good look—because this is the only chance you'll
get."

Mike glanced at him in surprise, then at the crystal.
"Looks ordinary enough to me. No—wait a minute—it's
beginning to glow in the centre!"

The centre of the crystal, seemingly some kind of silvery
metal no bigger than a small pea, was already like a red-
hot coal. As they watched the red glow whitened.

"It's as though it were absorbing the light of the sun into itself," G.B. exclaimed, "concentrating it in one tiny
spot of brilliance!"

Mike's eyes were already watering with the strain of
looking at it, but the brilliant spot went on brightening
until the whole crystal was a mass of white light in Dan's
hand—almost awe-inspiring in its fierce intensity.

Mike collapsed on a stool, mopping his eyes. "Phew—that's enough for me!"

Dan closed his fingers over the crystal to put it back in the box—and the light shone through him, showing up his bones almost like an X-ray.

G.B. frowned at the closed lid. "I've never seen anything like it!"

"Nor has anyone else, except an obscure tribe of Andean Indians." Dan perched on the bench, his fingers resting on the box lid. "As you know, the Indians of South America have dozens of legends, and one of the two most persistent concerns a 'light-which-never-goes-out'. For years Indians off the beaten track—not that there are many beaten tracks in some parts of South America!—have reported seeing strange lights. You may remember Col. Fawcett discussed them in his papers, as recently as the twenties." Mike nodded. "But primitive Indian ideas of distance and direction are so vague that no one has ever been able to find out anything definite, and the whole thing has been put down to superstition. But all the versions of the legend have certain features in common: the light is unquenchable, and more brilliant than any other light. It also leaves no trace of its burning—no smoke or grime. Keith and I believe this crystal contains a fragment of that 'light'."

"Seems to fit," Mike agreed. "But what is it actually?"

"In itself, it's not really remarkable from an analytical point of view," said Dan. "It's a substance similar to radium, of volcanic origin."

"How did Keith find it?" said G.B.

"We've been interested in the legend for some long time," Dan smiled slightly; "but we had other things to think about. As you know, our job didn't end until some while after the War. Well, Keith stayed out there, and I came home with the first crates from a dig near Cuzco. To cut a long story short, one of the old Spanish manuscripts I translated soon after my arrival home mentioned the 'light' as a fact, and indicated that a certain tribe knew where it was to be found. Keith, as I do, always believed that really persistent legends have one small grain of truth somewhere in them, however deep down, and thought it might be worth looking into. So he and John Akobe, and a third man who tagged on to Keith at Lima, took a trip into the interior to find this tribe. The Marubi."

"Who was this third chap?" said Mike. "And why did he tag on?"

"Oh, you know how these things happen when you're on an expedition of this kind. Englishmen in a foreign country, birds of a feather, and so on. He was just a fellow enthusiast—with a very interesting sideline in vulcanology. He certainly knew what he was talking about. Keith wasn't too keen on him, but he couldn't penalize him for that: so he joined the party. John Akobe, you know best what happened then."

The African inclined his head in assent, and his deep voice took up the story.

"We travelled a great distance through the forest to the village of the Marubi. They were a friendly people, and welcomed us, and the headman told us readily of the light-which-never-goes-out, and of the 'great ones' to whom it belongs. But he could say nothing of where they might be found."

G.B.'s eyes narrowed. "'Could' or 'would'?"

"It was a sacred knowledge, for the headman alone. Our companion reacted badly—he had caught the greed-disease, Mike!" the African smiled. "Then Keith put the headman in his debt by saving the headman's young son from snakebite. The headman paid his debt by making Keith a blood-brother, and by sharing the sacred knowledge with him, of the way to 'the place of the great ones in the growling mountain'."

Mike chuckled. "I guess the other chap didn't like that!"

"No—though at first he hid it very well. Keith was away alone for thirty days—no one could go with him, of course, without the sacred knowledge. When he came back he brought the crystal which he asked me to bring to Dan. He told me to guard it carefully because it held power for both good and evil. Then he went back to the 'sacred place' and I came back through the forest."

"What happened to the other man?" said Mike

"He tried to follow Keith, but the Marubi were too ready for him. So he followed me. He tried to buy the crystal—although he didn't know exactly what it was that I carried. Then he tried to rob me while I slept."

"But John Akobe doesn't sleep!" Dan smiled.

"No. Then at the airfield the good God finally delivered me from him."

G.B. raised a startled eyebrow, and glanced at Mike.

"How?" said Mike.

"There was one plane, and one seat, so it was given to the white man." It was a simple statement of unresented fact. "Fourteen days passed before I could follow. I didn't see him again."

"And you think God arranged that?" said G.B. dryly.

John Akobe smiled. "I know He did."

G.B. shrugged and let it pass without comment, though Mike knew what he was thinking. They had argued often enough over the past six months for him to know G.B.'s views on such things!

Dan took up the thread again. "John Akobe arrived with the crystal, and that was that."

"Keith said power for good and evil," Mike reflected. "I can guess the good—I suppose it would be pretty useful as a source of illumination, if nothing else: but what's the evil?"

A bluebottle buzzed loudly on the sunlit window.

"As I told you," said Dan, "it's a substance similar to

radium, but—it's just as lethal as radium in the wrong dosage. I'll show you: a section of the crystal insulation comes away."

The "pea" had faded to a dull glow in the darkness of the cashbox, and began to blaze again at once when Dan lifted out the crystal. On the far, now exposed, side Mike could see a bluish tinge in the light. From where he sat, six feet away. Dan turned the "light" on the bluebottle. Its buzz stopped abruptly; and it fell with a small "plop".

Dan carefully replaced the crystal section, and put it away again.

Mike could think of nothing suitable to say.

"I think G.B. is probably right when he says it absorbs the sun into itself," Dan went on. "It seems to be simply a powerful natural force, reacting to light—it's totally inactive in darkness—which kills by a kind of radioactivity without destroying the tissues."

Mike had an unwelcome thought.

"Could it damage anything—er—bigger than that bluebottle?" he said.

"I stopped at a large rat," said Dan.

No one spoke for a moment.

"But you think it could kill a man." G.B. spoke Mike's thoughts with his customary bluntness.

"I have no doubt at all."

"Did this other chap know what it could do?" said Mike.

Dan shrugged. "The Marubi tradition was pretty accurate, as far as it went. I wondered if he might turn up here—Keith told him of our partnership—but he hasn't." He stood up suddenly. "The 'great ones'— whoever they are!—insisted on Keith's solemn promise that it would be destroyed as soon as we had studied it. I think they knew what they were doing! Few civilized men could be trusted with its possibilities: they're not held back by superstition or sacred tradition like the primitive races. It would be a magnet to every crook going!"

"Have they any more?" said G.B.

"I understand the only portable piece is incorporated in some kind of ceremonial mask or other, and protected by the tradition I mentioned. It's most probably just a freak caused by volcanic eruption—an unusual fusion of certain elements under tremendous heat. Of course," he added, "it goes without saying that you won't mention this outside these four walls!"

Mike grinned. "We'd look a couple of Charlies if we did!"

"Have you any formula or records of it?" said G.B.

"They're in the safe. But they're harmless so long as no one knows exactly where to find the substance. And only the Marubi can put them on the way to it."

He poured some clear liquid carefully into the earthenware bowl. G.B.'s eyebrows shot up.

"You're not really going to destroy it!"

Mike sensed a sudden spark of antagonism between the two. Dan said nothing for a moment.

"It all depends," he said at last, deliberately replacing the glass stopper in the jar, "on whether man's integrity is of more value than mere scientific power, if one has to choose." His cold blue eyes challenged G.B. "Personally, I think it is!"

G.B. met him shrewdly for a moment, then apparently decided to keep his thoughts to himself.

Mike tried to snap the potential atmosphere. "How are you going to do it?"

"In this solvent. It won't touch the rock crystal, so it will still be insulated if my formula doesn't work as it should! Phew—I shan't really be sorry when this is over!" Dan smiled grimly. "It's the hottest stuff I've ever had to handle!"

He turned the crystal and slipped away the loose

section. The clear liquid became a blazing sea of gold fire so long as any of the inner substance remained. Then the fire suddenly went out.

Dan gazed abstractedly at the cloudy solution for a moment.

"Absolute destruction is so—final, isn't it?" he murmured.

He poured all the liquid carefully down the lab. drain. "Put the solvent back on the shelf, Mike, out of harm's way," he said over his shoulder.

Mike lifted his hand, too quickly and awkwardly, and knocked his wrist hard against the underside of the bench.

"Broken it?" said Dan, as Mike listened anxiously to his watch. "Lay it down for a while: might steady it."

They were almost at Dan's flat before Mike remembered the watch again.

"It's all right: you all go on," he urged. "I'll get a bus back. I won't be long."

The Museum was still open, but there were very few visitors in the galleries. It was eerily quiet on the top floor: the offices were deserted by this time, and the cleaners had not yet arrived.

Mike unlocked Dan's office door, and stood still suddenly, his nerves tingling.

He hadn't exactly heard anything, but some sixth sense warned him the rooms weren't empty.

He opened the door a crack. There was no one in the office. He walked softly across to the laboratory door and listened.

Someone was moving.

Mike turned the handle silently. A man in attendant's uniform was bending over the open safe looking rapidly and expertly through some papers. Mike couldn't see his face, but the thick leather glove on the crippled left hand was unmistakable.

"Jackson! What d'you think you're doing!"

Jackson swung round, and without hesitation leapt at Mike. Unprepared for attack from the crippled attendant, Mike went down under him. Knees in his chest squashed the breath out of him, and two steel hands gripped his throat, forcing his head back. Gasping for breath Mike tore desperately at the fingers squeezing his windpipe. Dimly through throbbing redness he remembered a trick Dan had taught him. He gripped Jackson's little fingers, pulling them back with all his remaining strength. The right one cracked. The other crumpled in his hand like a piece of sponge. . . .

Then he fell into a bottomless black pit.

2

ACCIDENT PRONE

MIKE rested his pounding head in his hands.

"Yes, Dan, yes!—I'm quite sure! The little finger of his left hand was made of rubber!" He swallowed painfully. "Thank goodness you wondered where I'd got to and came back for me!"

Dan's face was grim. He reached for the telephone on his desk and dialled.

"I wouldn't have believed anyone could escape from that crash. I still don't know whether to believe it, but with a man like Gregory—Hello! Sir Henry? Brent here. Bad news, sir: I've reason to believe Matthew Gregory may not be as dead as we supposed! Yes ... Yes—that's part of the formula all right! I'll come at once. Goodbye."

"What's wrong, Dan?"

"He's already made an offer of the 'light'."

"Already? How do you know?"

"Radio message to a known foreign agent in this country. Gregory's usual method."

"Can't they trace it?"

"They have—to somewhere in Kensington Gardens! He's well away by now."

Mike wasn't too green to realize that the scarred eye, together with the paralysed side were no longer in existence.

"Can you make it to the car? You'd better come with me," said Dan briefly.

Sir Henry Brame, chief of Counter Espionage, listened

without comment as Dan told him of the potentialities of the "light".

"There can be no doubt at all that Jackson was Gregory," he said at last. "The offer of the substance by radio makes it absolutely certain. It seems most probable that the man who attached himself to Oban in Lima was also Gregory."

Dan's mouth tightened. "It's the kind of thing he would do—sheer bravado! Like the disguise he chose. A classic example of what a disguise shouldn't be. No doubt he regarded it as a challenge to his abilities! Though that eye was a clever stroke: it took all attention away from other details about him."

"How can he offer the 'light' if he hasn't got it?" said Mike.

"There's an almost unbalanced egotistic streak in his brain," said Dan, "and he'll be quite sure he will get it. Gregory has the devil's own pride and self-confidence— and cleverness to match. In his own eyes—and in a good many others' as well—he is unstoppable. Every government knows from bitter experience that if Gregory offers a thing he'll produce it. It's a point of honour with him, if such a blighter knows the meaning of the word!"

"So you think he'll make for the source of supply now," said Mike.

"We know he will." Sir Henry regarded Dan steadily beneath wiry grey brows. "He must be stopped, Brent. We have not discussed to whom he made the offer. It was to a Communist Power. I need not tell you what failure would mean to the morale—at the least—of this country. The propaganda value of the substance in their hands could be disastrous. They wouldn't need to falsify over this," he added dryly.

"May I have a free hand as before, Sir Henry?"

The steel grey eyes twinkled for a second, but his acknowledgement was as brief as Dan's acceptance of the commission.

"Thank you, Brent." He took a stiff, crested paper from the wall safe and wrote for a few minutes in a bold, firm hand.

Dan folded the paper and put it in a pocket of his jacket which Mike had never even suspected.

"Whom do you wish to assist you?"

Dan reflected. "I think the fewer who know of this the better. Oban is already there. I'll start at once—and pray I get there first."

With a grave nod of acquiescence Sir Henry picked up the telephone. "I will make arrangements for the inoculations at once."

Dan grimaced. "Drastic?"

A ghost of a smile twitched the other's mouth. "Drastic."

Dan said very little on the journey back to the flat. Mike thought it best to keep quiet and watch points. He had never seen this tight-lipped, singleminded, man-hunting side of Dan before, and didn't quite know how to tackle it.

It was John Akobe who spoke the question in Mike's mind.

"Is it wise to go alone, Dan?"

Dan moved methodically round the flat, collecting items of travelling equipment.

"Nothing else for it. In a job of this kind I must know the man I'm working with. In any case the fewer lives risked the better."

"Will it come to that?" said G.B., frowning.

Dan laughed briefly. "It's the one sure thing about it!"

"A zebra running alone is no match for the lion—but if two run together one will escape," John Akobe quoted.

Dan smiled. "Thanks, John Akobe. I can't deny that —but I have no right to ask you to risk being the one who doesn't escape."

G.B. broke in with the occasional high-handed tone which never failed to make Mike see red.

"I'd say that neither have you the right to let so

much depend on you alone when others are prepared to lessen the risk!"

The spark jumped between them again, and a flush crept up Dan's stiff face.

"This is no child's game of cops and robbers!" he snapped.

Mike forestalled G.B.'s retort. "I think G.B.'s right this time, Dan. I think we all know what sort of a game it is—" he touched his bruised throat ruefully: "—I do, anyway. And none of us are children. And we know as well as you that it's more than just politics. If those blighters ever got a hold on things we could say goodbye to everything we've ever valued or believed in as Englishmen—and Christians! I agree with John Akobe as well: and what's true of two can be more true of three or four. With you on your own Gregory's only got to engineer a convenient accident, and he has a clear field. Four of us would present a bigger problem—and the chances of getting through would be times four if he decided to tackle us one by one!" Mike suddenly felt embarrassed at his outburst. "I'm sorry, Dan: I—I know I'm trying to teach my grandmother to suck eggs: but if your only objection is the risk to our safety——"

Dan frowned at him thoughtfully.

"Young Mike is right, Dan. 'The quarry is of more value than the hunters'."

John Akobe's gently spoken observation seemed to decide Dan, though Mike knew his mind had been working at top speed. Dan looked at them grimly, each in turn.

"Right," he said at last; "the quarry *is* worth more than the hunters, and you seem to have some kind of an idea of what you'll be up against. But I want it clearly understood that you obey orders. And if I should be put out of the running John Akobe takes over."

Mike's heart beat painfully in his aching throat with an excited apprehension. "That's O.K. by me."

G.B. was cool and unmoved as usual. "I agree."

"I, too, agree."

Suddenly Dan grinned. "Now I've saddled myself with you I'll have to make the best of it, I suppose. But thanks, anyway," he added gruffly. "Now then, jump to it! We report to the hospital in half an hour with night gear."

"Hospital!" Mike and G.B. echoed.

"Even Sir Henry can't get us in without the proper inoculation certificates," said Dan. "Gregory may get in illegally, but we can't! We may need Government co-operation."

During the next two days Mike fervently wished he had never been born. On the third day the disastrous effects of the speeded-up inoculations quickly wore off. On the fourth morning they returned to the flat to find John Akobe and their travelling kit ready and waiting.

Dan looked at his watch. "O-eight-hundred hours. That gives us fifteen minutes before Sir Henry comes with our papers. All set, John Akobe? Did you find every-thing all right?"

"I did not find G.B.'s Bible," said John Akobe, "so I packed a spare one from the bookcase for him."

Dan nodded. "Good. Then we'll commit ourselves and the job to God and we'll be ready to go."

As Mike expected, G.B. wandered away to the window while they knelt on the hearthrug, but no one passed any comment; though Mike caught a faintly surprised glance from Dan.

"I need not emphasize the absolute necessity for suc-cess," were Sir Henry's last grave words to them, as they shook hands at the London Airport.

The flight to Sao Paulo was uneventful, smooth—and fast.

"Afraid there's no time to look round!" said Dan as they freshened up in their small hotel room. "We spend this afternoon collecting the rest of our equipment, then it's an early night. Our plane leaves at three in the morning."

Mike mopped his scarlet face. "I'll be glad to get into some shorts," he panted. "This heat flattens me!"

"Shorts!" Dan chuckled. "As soon as we touch the forests every bare inch of skin will be a target for more stinging insects than you ever knew existed. You'll be glad to cover yourself up, my lad—britches, boots, hat— the lot! We won't be able to carry much. A couple of changes of clothing, medical supplies and food—and, of course, a rifle and revolver each. It isn't jaguar country, but you never know."

That evening in their room they held a briefing session. Dan re-checked travelling directions with John Akobe.

"Two days up the Red River to the Marubi village: they guide us to the sacred river, all being well! Then eight days up the sacred river to the 'place of white rocks'—exact nature unknown—and four days along the 'trail-where-nothing-grows' to the 'city of Xicchu' in the growling mountain—assumed to be some kind of semi-extinct volcano. And if one or more of us is put out of action, the rest carry on," he finished. "Time is absolutely vital. Gregory has three days' start, and we've got to make that time up somehow. He'll know we'll be on to him so he won't let the grass grow under him either. Get as much sleep as you can tonight. This is the last bed you'll see for some long time!"

Mike felt horribly conspicious and rather silly at two o'clock in the morning in "the lot", with pack, rifle and machete slung on his back, and snake serum in his breast pocket. His first sight of John Akobe did nothing to lessen the effect. He wore nothing but a loincloth, and carried his pack and a blanket native-wise, slung from his left shoulder. Mike noticed he had no rifle, only a long-bladed knife in a sheath on his right hip.

"I feel dressed again!" G.B. smiled, patting his well-polished barrel as they stood in the dark entrance waiting for their "taxi".

"I hear you're pretty good," said Dan.

Mike laughed. "He just can't miss!"

"What do you make the time, Mike?" Dan frowned at last. "A quarter to three?—so do I. The taxi's fifteen minutes late already."

It rolled up eventually, and no amount of persuasion would make the sleepy driver go any faster.

It was still quite dark when they arrived at their airfield, and Mike could just make out a small plane a couple of hundred metres distant from the main buildings. A dim uniformed figure approached, speaking in halting English.

"Senor Brent?"

"Hallo! Yes, I'm Brent. Are you our pilot? I'm sorry we ran it so close, but that——"

The stocky Spaniard waved agitated hands.

"Si, senor—it is all right, yes! You please to board, senors! No more long waits—no? I come, pronto!"

"Seems in rather a hurry!" said Mike, as they walked towards the plane. "It's our plane after all."

"That's what I thought," said Dan. "Mike, glance back and see if you can see him."

Mike took a casual look over his shoulder. "Seems to be standing looking after us. Now he's waving us on. Now he's gone back in the direction of the hangars as far as I can make out. I say, it is a bit late really, you know! We should have been well on board by now. Can't really blame him for getting a bit excited. Come on!"

Dan gripped his arm and held him back. "Not on your life!"

Suddenly the world blew up in Mike's face.

"Down!" yelled Dan.

Mike didn't need any telling. He twisted and flung himself on the gritty earth. The ground bucked, and something solid seemed to travel along his whole length, knocking the breath out of him. Then the bits of burning fuselage began dropping. He was dragged to his feet and forced into a run by John Akobe. Dan followed close behind with G.B. Nothing else exploded, and they halted in the shelter of the main buildings.

"As you say," said Dan grimly: "we should have been on board."

Mike felt suddenly sick in the pit of his stomach. He glanced at G.B. G.B.'s lips were tight, his face a white oval in the dimness. His eyes were fixed on the burning wreckage. Mike laughed shakily.

"I suppose we'd better get used to this kind of thing!"

The place was suddenly alive. Weird figures in the flickering light appeared from nowhere, all shouting and gesticulating frantically as they ran to and fro across the tarmac. Dan stood where he was and bellowed once for the Controller of the Airfield. The poor man's pale round head glistened as he wilted under Dan's non-stop flow of fluent Portuguese.

An hour later they were moving along the runway in a second plane personally inspected and passed by the Controller himself.

Mike eased off his pack and settled for the twenty-hour journey which was to bring them two thousand miles to their jumping-off point on the edge of civilization. He looked down at the carpet of treetops, unbroken for as far as he could see.

"Looking forward to hacking your way through them?" Dan laughed. "We refuel at Tres Lagoas on the Rio Parana, and again at Santa Cruz. I've arranged a change of pilot at each halt so we shan't lose any time by stopping for rest. It's rather close quarters in here, but we can snatch a few hours as we go."

Soon they were passing over the mist-covered forests and swamps of the Matto Grosso. Stretching far away to his right Mike caught glimpses of the blue-green expanse of the Amazon Basin, and here and there a glint of a river as it caught the morning sun. Five hundred km. to his left the chain of the Andes, snow-capped and majestic, appeared and disappeared through the clouds.

As they crossed the marshes and low-lying forest of the River Paraguai Mike caught sight of round thatched roofs in a clearing. He frowned at them thoughtfully.

"Brings it home, doesn't it?" Dan remarked. "We're really on our way."

"Do you think Xicchu will be like that?" Mike nodded towards the primitive village below.

"And just how 'great' are the 'Great Ones'?" smiled G.B.

"They were both 'huaca' to the Marubi." Dan glanced at John Akobe for confirmation.

"That's holy, or sacred, in Quechua, isn't it?" said G.B.

"In a way. They apply it to anything strange or unusual, but it has a superstitious tinge. At a guess I should say they are some fairly powerful tribe living in comparative isolation—either deep in the forest or somewhere in the mountains. That's not unusual, of course, but their isolation would add to their prestige in the eyes of a primitive people like the Marubi." Dan grimaced. "And they may have rough ways with anyone trying to enter their territory. That's not unusual either! There may be some such tribal memory among the Marubi, and discretion has gradually glorified itself into what some middle African tribes would call a taboo, so that the way to the territory is now a 'sacred secret'."

"But Keith went back again," Mike observed.

Dan frowned. "That's so. They couldn't have objected too roughly to him! You know—that's an intriguing factor of the whole thing to me: why he went back in such a hurry. But I expect the tribe was of some particular interest—and once he's on the trail of something there's no stopping him!"

By their second stop at Santa Cruz Mike had ceased to care, about tribes or anything else. He staggered out of the little plane to stretch his legs, only to stagger back again twenty minutes later. For the last lap of the journey he was too stiff to be impressed even by the grandeur of the dark purple mountains, their snowcaps rosy pink in the evening sun.

"We follow the mountains now to the landing field at Rio dos Barbaros," said Dan. "We'll get some sleep there."

The journey took much longer than Dan had hoped and they arrived at Rio dos Barbaros on the edge of the forest just twenty-eight hours after their departure from Sao Paulo.

Mike gazed appalled at the sun-baked scene of desolation, as nearly speechless as possible.

"This is just about the most miserable hole I've ever been in!"

G.B., too, seemed at a loss for words.

"The only thing to be said for it is the almost reasonable condition of the runway!" he exclaimed at last.

The place consisted entirely of beaten, baked earth, absolutely bare. To the far right stood three crazy wooden shacks of different sizes.

Mike grimaced. "Sleep?" he asked. "Where?"

Dan chuckled. "Come on. They may not be as bad as they look."

They hoisted their packs, and the young Portuguese pilot, almost out on his feet, went to look for signs of life.

From the smallest shack emerged a little Portuguese of the greasiest brand, followed by a skinny, almost hairless dog, which sniffed anxiously at their boots. The man's yellow teeth spread across his swarthy face in a grin of welcome.

"You are ver' welcome, senores! Come—Hernando make you ver' comfortable! You come, please!" He backed away bowing and washing his grimy hands. "Come, senores!"

He led them to the middle shack and bowed them in with great ceremony. He waved a hand round the filthy room.

"Please to make yourselves comfortable. I bring food

—you not wish food?" in answer to Dan's hasty exclamation. "Drink then! You thirsty!"

"Gasping," Mike muttered.

"I bring drink. Chaco?—coffee?" He hastened away to fetch the coffee.

"At least the water will be boiled!" Dan remarked grimly. "We can let it cool."

Mike stared round him and shuddered. He was about to dump his pack on the floor, but he thought better of it, though the table was little improvement. He sat down warily on one of the wooden stools.

Dan knocked an evil-looking beetle off the table. "I didn't think you'd fancy his food!"

The scrawny mongrel pounced on the beetle and swallowed it.

Hernando returned with a steaming jug and four mugs, which he placed carefully on the table. He bowed himself away as far as the door and stood looking at them.

"It is hot, Hernando," Dan assured him. "We wish to let it cool."

He seemed satisfied, and, snarling savagely at the dog under his feet, disappeared.

Mike rested an elbow gingerly on the table and stretched his legs.

G.B. scowled. "That hound could do with a good meal —or else a bullet through the head."

Mike mopped his neck. "That steam doesn't help the atmosphere!" He looked across at the pilot, dead to the world on a bunk in the dim recesses of the shack. "He's the happiest of us at the moment, I should think."

Dan inspected the jug. "I wouldn't touch the mugs with a barge-pole, but the jug looks fairly reasonable."

Mike sat and looked at the jug until he could bear it no longer.

"I expect it's cool enough now! I've got all my moisture outside at the moment!" He leaned over the jug and sniffed "My hat—it's strong! And no milk or sugar

either! Ugh!" He picked up the jug by the body and promptly dropped it again. "Ouch—that's hot!"

Dan dived to save it, but not before a good part had poured on to the floor.

"Good old Mike!" murmured G.B. "Come on, hound; it's a pity to waste it. You'll probably find a few more beetles in it!"

The dog needed no second calling. He sidled in, eyeing them warily.

Mike watched it gulping at the hot black liquid, its skin hardly covering its bones.

Suddenly it bounded to one side. It stood trembling for a moment, then its legs gave way. It rolled on the floor jerking in violent convulsions. They quickly lessened, and, with a final twitch, it lay still.

They all stared at it, dumbfounded, Mike clinging to the jug handle. G.B. drew a deep breath, and got up slowly.

He soon arrived at his verdict.

"Yes, it's dead."

3

WORD OF HONOUR

MIKE suddenly let go of the jug.

Dan picked it up and smelt it. "Coffee's too strong to smell anything else." He looked at the dog. "It's just possible a creature in that state may have died naturally. We'll soon find out! Draw the table over the splash, and put the dog out of sight—don't touch it with your hands whatever you do!"

He went to the door and called. The little Portuguese hurried across from his hut and stood in the doorway, smiling and stooping.

"The senor calls?" His eyes flickered to the jug on the table.

"Yes, Hernando," said Dan pleasantly, waving him in. "Come and share our coffee with us. You must be glad of a little company!"

"I thank you, no, senor! It is ver' kind—but Hernando already have plenty to drink——!"

"I can imagine that!" Mike muttered, screwing up his nose.

"No, Hernando, I will not accept a refusal. Come, we are your guests!"

Hernando's smile disappeared, and he backed away. "No, I thank you——"

"Grab him, John Akobe!" snapped Dan, "and keep him quiet! We don't want the pilot in this!"

Struggling and mumbling under John Akobe's hand the Portuguese was hauled to the table. Dan lifted the jug to his mouth.

"No—no—!" John Akobe cut off his scream of terror, and wide black eyes stared glassily over the top of his hand.

"All right, out with it!" Dan's voice was stony. "Who paid you?"

The greasy head shook vigorously. "No one pay me, senor!" he gasped.

"Oh, so it was your own idea!"

"No—I mean—no, senor!" Tears of helpless terror flowed down the swarthy cheeks. The Portuguese sagged in John Akobe's hold. "No—I no tell!"

"He's been frightened more than paid," Dan muttered. "Gregory's expert at both methods." He confronted the cringing man. "Shall I tell you who paid you, Hernando?" he said smoothly. The swimming eyes stared at him. Dan held up his left hand, back outwards and fingers spread. Then he deliberately bent his little finger at the bottom joint. The Portuguese seemed to go frantic with terror. He struggled wildly, the sweat rolling down his face.

"All right, let him go," said Dan. As soon as John Akobe's support was withdrawn the man collapsed on the floor. He half scrambled to his feet and went running and stumbling out of the shack.

"What now?" said Mike. "I suppose at least it shows we're on the right track!"

"But he's still ahead," observed G.B.

"He will be," said Dan. "We'll have to make up our time in the forest."

"We'd better get on then, hadn't we?" said Mike, picking up his pack.

Dan smiled. "We're not supermen! We'll have to sleep some time! We'll aim to start out at five: that will give us a good six hours. We'll meet the mosquitoes, but we can't help that. You three get some rest. I'll keep watch for our friend—though I think he's almost as frightened of us as of Gregory now!"

"No—I don't need to sleep yet," said John Akobe. "I will take first watch."

"Right-ho. Thanks, John Akobe. We'll turn in then. The bunks don't look very appetizing—but whatever you do, don't pull them any closer to the wall! What are you smiling at, G.B.?"

"I was just thinking," said G.B. "Do I understand that God's protection—which I have heard about from Mike —doesn't stretch to Portuguese would-be poisoners?"

"Not at all," said Dan evenly; "it's just that He doesn't often do things for us that we can perfectly well do for ourselves."

G.B. flushed slightly, and Dan glanced quizzically at Mike.

"We've been arguing for six months," Mike grinned. "I ought to have warned you, Dan! He won't budge. Neither will I, for that matter!"

Dan laughed. "I see! Well, it's just as well to know where we stand!"

Mike approached his bunk gingerly.

"I think I'll sleep on the floor!" he announced when he saw it.

"You won't!" said Dan. "The other bugs, beetles and what-have-you of various kinds wouldn't like it. Cover yourself up and hope for the best, Mike!"

Mike lay down on the filthy canvas with his face to the wall. What he saw there wasn't encouraging, so he lay on his back. The roof was dark and held too many possibilities, so he rolled on to his other side with his hat pulled down, and turned his collar up.

He knew nothing more till he woke to find the others strapping on their packs.

"Pilot went three hours ago," said Dan, "and our friend is sleeping off a couple of jugs of chaco. If we're all ready we'll make tracks. Due west from here to the Red River, then we follow it up to a sharp left bend where the Marubi village is."

The forest rose abruptly from the edge of the airfield. Mike was looking forward to escaping from the broiling sun, but he wasn't sure that the exchange was to his advantage.

The thick, damp heat rolled up at him from the forest floor, soaking him at once with sweat which wouldn't evaporate. His feet lost themselves in a tangle of fleshy growth, and after a while the forest seemed to bear down on him, purposely tripping him, catching his face and arms with hanging, coiling tentacles. Every movement was soon an effort, leaving him deadly weary.

In the perpetual green twilight the tall straight trees were pale and ghostly, but here and there a gold shaft of sunlight struck through the solid roof of tree-tops on to the floor of ferns and fleshy leaves.

Now and again a splash of incredible purple or flame orchids broke the green high above their heads, and iridescent humming birds no more than two inches long hovered on invisible wings, changing direction suddenly in mid-flight, and darting away again. Butterflies with a twelve-inch wing-span flickered by, like blue neon lights.

A troop of monkeys chattered across the tree-tops, knocking down small fruit over them. Bright bronze beetles scurried away across the rotting timber of fallen trees, and furry-legged spiders glided up tree trunks. Over everything hung a sickly rotten smell which stuck in Mike's throat for a while. It was worse on low-lying ground, where they stirred up pools of stagnant water, each with its own cloud of insects.

After two hours' exhausting hacking and stumbling they struck the river, flowing through a green tunnel.

Mike considered it. Not very wide, no more than ten metres, it flowed along fairly leisurely. Broad patches of slow-moving dull red weed showed clearly how it got its name.

"Shouldn't be too difficult to ascend," G.B. observed.

Mike looked up at the inseparable green tangle ten or fifteen metres overhead, and shuddered.

"Makes you feel pinned down!" he exclaimed.

"You'll get used to it," Dan smiled. "We'll build a raft: it will be quicker than struggling along the banks."

There was plenty of material—young trees, and lianas like rope. John Akobe took the first turn at punting, and Mike sat at the ready, watching the mighty, effortless strokes, and the muscles rippling under the gleaming black skin.

"No sign of any Indians," Mike remarked after a while.

"Each tribe has its own territory," said Dan: "and most of them keep away from the rivers. The whites have treated them unbelievably badly, and they've gone deeper into the forests. Which is probably just as well for us. They carry the memory of an injury for generations, and take their revenge on the next white man they meet. Some of the fiercer tribes will kill on sight. Others, like the Marubi I'm glad to say, are gentler and more peaceable, and will only kill if really pushed to it to defend themselves. They'll never take the initiative and attack, without extreme provocation."

It was growing too dark to see, so they made the raft fast and camped for the night on a small beach. Apart from his two-hour watch Mike found the night passed quickly, and his hammock considerably more comfortable than the bunk of the previous night.

About the middle of the second morning they sighted the left bend, and John Akobe skilfully poled the raft across-stream to the wide curving beach.

Mike felt a thrill of excitement. Something concrete at last—the first real stage of the journey was over! Now they had only to make contact with their guides and they were as good as there. Dan had no doubts of their co-operation, apparently. If the fiercer Indians remembered an injury, tribes like the Marubi also remembered the opposite, and John Akobe believed they would rise to helping Keith against Gregory. Mike sincerely hoped so!

The raft was halfway across, and Mike knelt up ready to jump off, when there was a shrill bird-call from behind the trees, and a shower of heavy arrows thudded into the raft and sheared the water all round them.

"Back, John Akobe!" shouted Dan. "Mercifully they seem poor shots!" he added. The raft sped back across the red water, followed by a second irregular volley. They leapt ashore, dragging the raft up, and dashed for the cover of the trees. Dan snapped off an arrow as he ran.

They held a council of war at a safe distance from the river.

"Have we made a mistake?" said Mike. "They don't look very peaceable and gentle to me!"

"No: this is a Marubi arrow, all right." Dan indicated a snake scratched on the arrow shaft. "And that wasn't a soldierly offensive. No, something's happened to turn or frighten them."

"Gregory again?" said G.B.

"Little doubt of that," said Dan grimly. "But whatever it is, we've got to have their help. Humanly speaking we're helpless without them."

"They were bound to Keith by blood," John Akobe said thoughtfully, "and looked on me as his servant. I will show myself to them—"

"Thanks, John Akobe, but no," said Dan firmly. "In their state they'll shoot first and recognize you afterwards."

G.B. was fingering his rifle. "At this range I could easily bring down one or two of them," he remarked. "That ought to scare them."

"And that of course would encourage them to help us!" Dan snapped. "In any case, that's not the way we do things! There'll be no shooting unless it's absolutely necessary, and then not to kill."

G.B. shrugged. "If you say so."

"No," said Dan. "The best plan is for us all to go together, and make it very plain that we come in peace."

"Sitting ducks," Mike observed.

"What else do you suggest, then?" said Dan. "We must

make contact with them somehow, and soon! Don't forget that Gregory is still three days ahead."

"That's true," said Mike.

"They're not killers by nature," Dan went on. "We know that. If we take it slowly, and assure them we mean them no harm, I think our chances are pretty even."

"Good," said John Akobe briefly.

Mike pursed his lips dubiously. "All right. As there doesn't seem to be any other way."

"I think it's near lunacy," said G.B. coolly; "but I don't propose to stay here on my own. I agree."

"Right," said Dan. "John Akobe will punt across slowly. As soon as we are in clear view we'll lay down our rifles behind us, and go on with clearly empty hands. Then John Akobe will tell them that we hate killing as they do, and that we come in peace seeking their help against a man with three fingers who is evil. If Gregory has been before us they'll remember a peculiarity like that— unless he disguised his hand as he did the first time. We'll take our cue from what happens then. But, remember, no resistance unless I give the word!"

They emerged from the shelter of the trees.

"Now, look confident, even if you don't feel it!" said Dan.

They reached the raft with no sign from the Indians, and pushed off on to the narrow strip of red water. In midstream John Akobe steadied the raft and hailed them in the Quechua dialect. Mike strained his eyes at the trees, but there was no sign or movement. There was complete silence except for the calling and chattering of the wild life, and the lapping of the water. John Akobe called again, and gave them Dan's message. There was still no sign.

"Right. Lay down your rifles as obviously as you can."

Mike's heart thumped. Still no sign from the bank.

"They're waiting till we land!" G.B. muttered.

The raft crunched on the beach—and immediately

they were surrounded by a semicircle of slight, lightbrown Indians, each with a loaded bow poised.

"Greetings, people of the Marubi," said Dan gravely in Quechua. "We come in peace."

An elderly, straight-backed Indian, whom Mike took to be the headman, detached himself from the others. He came forward a few paces and made a brief gesture. At once the others raised their bows.

G.B. dived for his rifle, and was on his knee aiming at the headman before anyone could move. Mike kicked the barrel up and the shot smacked into the trees over the Indian's head, sending up a squawking flurry of birds.

"You blithering idiot!" Dan grabbed the rifle and flung it back on the raft, but it was too late. With a yell the Indians were on them. They were bound swiftly and hauled away up the beach to the forest.

Mike eyed the Indians apprehensively as he stumbled along the trail. They had the typical high cheekbones and short black fringe of the Indian, but they were more finely made and healthier looking than Mike had expected. Probably because they hadn't been in touch with white civilization, he reflected. But they had their own degree of civilization: their bark-cloth clothes—though no more elaborate than John Akobe's—were skilfully dyed. They were clearly not warriors, and followed their headman in an untidy file, exclaiming and gesticulating with arms and bows.

The village was comparatively large, with twenty or more shallow cone-shaped huts dotted about a sun-baked clearing in the forest. So this was what they looked like from the ground. . . .

The procession crossed the village to one of three larger huts, followed by an inquisitively chattering crowd of brown women and children, and old men.

The chief seated himself with a kind of simple dignity on a low stool and considered them. Then he addressed John Akobe.

"You come in peace, black man? Yet he—" he pointed to G.B. "—he brings the blow-pipe speaking thunder and death to my people."

John Akobe bowed his head. "Yet we come in peace, O chief whose heart is upright. He is but a boy, and as yet not wise in the ways of the brown men. Pardon him."

G.B. opened his mouth.

"Shut up!" hissed Dan.

The chief looked at John Akobe for a long moment as though trying to remember something. Then with no apparent relevance he said:

"My people worship the god of fire who dwells yonder." He raised a hand towards the scorching sun.

Mike glanced at Dan, wondering where the conversation was going, but John Akobe seemed to understand, and with an expressionless face made his answer.

"I and my brothers worship a greater God Who made the god of fire, O chief. He Who is the God of our brother, Keith."

"And how is this God named, black man who calls upon the name of my brother?"

"He is called Jesus."

To Mike's surprise and relief the chief smiled, and raised a hand.

"We salute and welcome you, John Akobe: you are ever our brother." He gestured towards the others. "But these I know not. The white man is not friend to the Marubi. His speech is not straight. His lips speak one thing, but his heart another. It is but two days since he with three fingers came." Mike met Dan's eye. "He, too, came in peace, but his pipe spoke to my second son, and he died. Then he spoke smooth words to my first son who held the sacred knowledge of my people. My first son followed him from the village, and has not returned."

Dan broke his silence.

"He who spoke false words is our enemy, O chief. We who worship the God called Jesus speak true words. He with three fingers does not so worship, nor does he so speak."

The headman considered him for a moment, then made a signal. They were immediately led away out of earshot, while the headman spoke to the now freed John Akobe. A second signal brought them back again.

The chief addressed Dan without any preamble.

"You say, white man, that they who worship the God called Jesus speak true words."

"That is so, O chief."

"They also have a word—a word which once given cannot be broken?"

Dan inclined his head in a slight bow of assent.

"Give me this word, white man, that you will not try to escape, and you shall be kept without bonds and shall go your way when our god appears yet again yonder." He pointed to the tree-tops behind them.

Mike looked at Dan in surprise, but Dan showed no sign of what he was thinking. G.B.'s eyes narrowed suspiciously.

Dan bent his head slightly again and they withdrew a few feet.

"John Akobe must have satisfied him about us," said Dan softly. "I don't know why he wants to keep us. It will mean another day, of course," he added, "if we do give our word."

"What's the alternative?" said Mike.

Dan frowned. "I don't know. But we mustn't let them think they're forcing us to anything."

"I agree there," G.B. muttered. "We've got to keep the upper hand, psychologically anyway."

"Exactly," Dan nodded. "And it means that other day in any case, as far as I can see; and there seems no logic in spending the night trussed up like this. Are you prepared to play along with them?"

Mike nodded. "Right-ho."

"And you, G.B.?"

"Nothing else for it."

They returned to the headman.

"We who worship the God called Jesus give you our word, O chief."

"It is good." The headman gave the order for them to be released, and they were taken to one of the larger huts and left, with a plentiful supply of smoked meat and juicy, though unidentifiable, fruit.

Mike enjoyed his first good sleep since he left England, and woke early the next morning.

"They weren't prepared to trust us!" Dan smiled. "There were two of them outside all night."

After breakfast they settled to wait for their release.

"That's the twentieth time you've peered through that hole, Mike!" said Dan some hours later.

Mike looked at his watch. "But it's eleven o'clock! We should have been out by now! And all they've done is bring us breakfast! If we don't get out of here soon it's going to be pretty plain sailing for Gregory. He must be almost halfway there by now!"

Their spirits rose when two Indians brought in their packs, but the Indians only shook their heads when Dan tried to question them.

Mike looked at his watch every ten minutes until it was too dark to see. He lay on his mat staring up at the black roof, an angry helplessness fuming inside him. The Indians had tricked them! He felt rotten, too. He'd never get hardened to being let down.

When at last he did sleep he was awakened by a movement in the hut.

"What on earth——! G.B.! What's going on?" He squinted at the tropical brightness of a star shining through a small hole in the roof.

"Quiet!" G.B. hissed. "I'm trying to see how strong the hut is." He packed the leaves back into the hole and came and squatted by Mike. "Listen, Mike. This place is only leaves woven together with lianas and mud. Some seem rather tough, but I think a good knife could make a hole big enough—though we'd have to find the best place to begin operations."

Mike stared at him, and G.B. frowned. "Look here, Mike," he whispered irritably. "I hope you're not going to talk any rubbish about not trying to get away. Every hour we stay here Gregory is getting a bigger advantage. It's a question of time, Mike! He was two days ahead at least yesterday: now it's three again. It's an eight-day journey up the 'sacred river'. As it is we stand a chance of stopping him—but another day and we might as well pack up and go home! I should think it's almost dawn. If they don't let us go this morning I'm taking the first chance that comes." He tapped Mike's chest. "Think about it, laddie."

Before Mike could answer, G.B. crossed the hut softly and lay down on his own mat.

Mike stared hard at the black roof. G.B. was right: if they didn't get away soon it would be too late! And there was no doubt at all that Gregory would hand over the "light": patriotism wasn't his strong point! They just *had* to get there first!

Dan produced a ray of hope when the morning had come and gone.

"It's possible they've let John Akobe go."

"Afraid not," said G.B. tersely. He was peering through a chink in the wall. "He's just gone into the chief's hut."

"Then we'll just have to wait in faith," said Dan finally and unexpectedly. "The Lord knows the situation better than we do."

Mike caught a look of absolute contempt as G.B. turned away. And he wasn't too sure himself.

Towards evening the two Indians appeared again, but again refused to answer Dan's questions. They laid the rifles and revolvers on the floor and went out in exasperating silence.

G.B. snatched up his rifle and feverishly checked it over. He gave an involuntary mutter of satisfaction.

"Still loaded!"

Dan took a last look outside before they lay down for the night, and smiled ruefully.

"They've paid us the compliment of not posting the guard tonight! What a pity we gave our word!"

Mike lay still, waiting for G.B. to move. At last he came and touched Mike on the shoulder.

"Mike!"

"I'm awake!" Mike whispered back.

"Have you thought it over?"

"Yes!"

"Well?"

Mike didn't reply.

G.B.'s whisper grew more urgent. "Look here, Mike. They've played right into our hands! It couldn't be better." Then as Mike still didn't answer: "If you're squeamish about a promise given to savages—!"

Mike still said nothing.

"All right then!" Mike sensed that the never-ruffled G.B. was trying to keep his temper. "Let's put it this way —from your point of view. You think we're doing something God wants us to do? Then isn't it right to take a first-class opportunity to get on with it? Do you think He wants us to keep a promise given to heathens—who've already broken their word, remember!—when so much is at stake? Time's getting short, Mike."

Mike hesitated. Had God really given the means of getting on with it? There was absolutely nothing to stop them now. Gregory was well on with his journey: they might have just one last chance of beating him if they got away now. Surely a man could break his promise under such circumstances! And G.B. had voiced his own thoughts— the Indians hadn't kept their side of the bargain. They had let them down badly.

Mike made his decision suddenly, and got to his feet.

G.B. picked up his pack and rifle. "I'm going to find

John Akobe. We'll have to force the headman to guide us. Are you coming then, after all? Good lad!"

"No—nor are you!"

G.B. stopped in the open doorway. "Oh?"

Mike slowly clenched his fists. "We gave them our word —as Christians, not just as white men."

G.B.'s teeth gleamed faintly in the dimness.

"But that hardly concerns me, does it? Mike, you're a fool! Be a realist! What good are religious principles in a thing like this? You can't beat men like Gregory with 'fair play'!"

"And you can't do God's work by evil means!"

"God's work—my eye! Anyhow, I'm not prepared to sit still and give Gregory a clear run, whoever's work it is! I suppose you realize that if he gets to this village, or city— or whatever it is—he's going to prepare the ground for us, just as he did here!"

"We'll have to take our chance on that."

G.B.'s sarcasm sizzled.

"And no doubt the Lord will provide! Well, I'm not waiting to find out. This is where we part company—and it's going to take more than faith to stop me!"

Mike filled his lungs and judged his distance as well as he could in the dimness.

"Sorry, G.B., nothing personal——"

A fist like a flying rock landed neatly to the side of G.B.'s jaw. With a surprised grunt he spun half round and col- lapsed.

"Sorry, G.B.—but it had to be done. If you'd only get it into your head that God isn't just a 'religious principle'!"

G.B. stayed out until just before dawn. Mike watched him as he slowly came round. He wasn't looking forward to their interview.

The heavy eyes wandered hazily round the hut, and at last focused on Mike's face. G.B. frowned and struggled to his elbow.

"What happened?"

To Mike's surprise G.B. took his explanation without a word.

"Yes—I remember now." He worked his jaw and winced. "I suppose I asked for it."

"Er—no hard feelings, then?"

G.B. looked at him curiously. "Not on my side, laddie. To tell you the truth, I didn't think you had it in you! But I'm still getting away at the first opportunity." And his mouth set hard again.

But G.B. wasn't given an opportunity. At dawn the headman sent for them and their equipment.

"The white men who worship the God called Jesus do indeed speak true words," he said. "The Marubi will help them. If they had not spoken true words they would have died," he added.

John Akobe gave a broad, triumphant smile, and suddenly Mike understood. It had been a test! He glanced at G.B. G.B. was scarlet to the hair-roots—then sickly pale. Probably at the realization of what he'd nearly done! They could hardly afford the setback, but at least they were alive—and on their way at last.

The headman's third son, deputed to lead them to the sacred river, walked ahead of them in a proud silence, his hammock slung over his left shoulder and his bow in his left hand. They must have been following a trail, though Mike couldn't see it, for they passed easily through the thick leaves, only having to cut at very new growth.

Once Mike felt a peculiar sensation—as though he were going to fall for no apparent reason. He looked at Dan to see if he had felt it.

"Earth tremor," Dan explained. "We're not far from the mountains here."

Late the following afternoon the Indian stopped suddenly, and pointed ahead.

"There lies the sacred river of the Great Inca. When the

white men wish to return let them send a smoke sign. I will come."

Without another word he turned back the way they had come, and before anyone could thank him he was swallowed up in the forest.

"The Great Inca, eh?" Dan exclaimed. "Now that's interesting!"

"Yes, but I can't see any river!" said Mike, looking round at the dense growth.

They found the river a few metres further on in a blaze of sunlight, as wide as the Thames at Westminster, and reflecting the deep blue of the open sky. In place of the Embankment were wide sloping beaches, with the trees rising dense and abrupt as usual.

Mike screwed up his eyes in the sudden light. There were no trees meeting overhead here. A brilliant orange and black toucan-like bird flapped heavily across with ear-piercing squawks, but evidently it was the wrong time to see much of the life of the river—except for columns of mosquitoes rising along the banks in preparation for their evening fun.

They set to at once to make a raft of the plentiful balsa wood.

"It's an eight-day journey up-river," said Dan. "If we travel at night as far as we can before the trees close in again we should make up some of the four days. John Akobe and I will take turns at night, and you two in the daytime. The things to look out for are snags—those nearly submerged logs like that one there! Some are rock hard and would probably come off best in a collision. And the other things are cayman. We'll probably meet those in the upper reaches. There may be anaconda as well, but I don't think they'll trouble us if we keep our eyes open."

Dan's advice was taken well to heart, and for the first three days and nights they made good progress. Then Mike noticed the river was beginning to narrow perceptibly, and to flow faster. The sides changed from monotonous beaches and walls of trees to steep banks, some undercut by the current, with tangled masses of fallen trees rotting at the water's edge. They had a narrow escape as one such mass detached itself from the bank just ahead and bore down on them. It was mainly John Akobe's strength which saved them from being caught up in it.

Dan considered it too dangerous to travel by night any further, so from then on they camped on the banks.

The river was becoming increasingly narrow and fast. It rushed between steep, rocky sides, and suitable camping places were few and far between. They had to portage several small waterfalls.

"Earth tremors are more noticeable here, aren't they!" Mike remarked as they made their way over the rocks.

"You can feel the vibration a good way away—according to their strength at source, of course," said Dan.

"Are there still active volcanoes in the Andes then?"

"Nothing of importance, except well to the north."

"What are these tremors then?"

"Oh, a volcano will rumble on for centuries sometimes, and nothing happens."

In the mid-morning of the eighth day Mike spotted their objective: a quay of once white stone, jutting into the river.

"That's it!" Dan agreed. "The place of white rocks. Forest Indians certainly wouldn't know the word for a jetty."

"Overgrown," Mike remarked. "I should say it stretches quite a way under that green stuff."

The jetty was almost hidden by a growth of creeping weeds and moss, but the steps leading down into the water was clearly discernible.

"Nippy mooring rings!" Mike exclaimed, as they poled nearer. "Looks from here as though the stone has been hollowed out behind, leaving a kind of column in front to tie the rope round. It all looks in pretty good shape, considering!"

"Considering what?" said G.B. dryly.

"Well, if this really is the Incas' river the jetty could be four hundred years old at least! What would you say, Dan?"

"I'd say it looks as though this trip is going to be interesting in more ways than one!" said Dan slowly. "If 'the trail where nothing grows' is any kind of a road—which I think it may be by that description—you can be sure the Incas really did have a finger in it!"

Even John Akobe found it difficult to manoeuvre the raft across the now racing river. He managed it after three unsuccessful attempts, and Dan slipped a liana through one of the mooring "rings".

"You all nip ashore and I'll hand up the packs," Mike volunteered, and hanging on to the slim stone bar with one hand he tried to steady himself on the rocking raft. He handed up the nearest revolver and bent to pick up a pack, when a sudden shout from Dan froze him.

"Mike! Leave it! Get ashore—don't stop for anything!"

Instinctively Mike looked round.

Not fifty metres away and bearing down on him with terrifying speed was a solid, foaming, plunging island of vegetation. For a second Mike was paralysed: the raft was tugging and leaping—he couldn't possibly get to the steps! Without stopping to think he grabbed at the stone bar with both hands and hung on with all his strength.

The next second the raft shot from under him.

4

TOWARDS THE GROWLING MOUNTAIN

THE wall of water had snapped the moorings like cotton.

Mike dropped to arm's length, up to his thighs in water. The rushing river washed over him, pulling at him, tugging his fingers from the bar. He was slipping— he'd hardly had time to get a grip! He kicked desperately against the current, his left hand jerked away and he was swung round by the force of the water, hanging on by his finger-ends. He clutched wildly at the stone with his left hand. . . .

Then his wrists were grasped, and he was being hauled bodily up the side of the jetty. The island crashed past, tearing away the creeper, and scraping the stone wall.

Mike lay on his back and gasped.

"Mike—are you all right?" Dan shook him.

He grinned feebly and struggled to sit up. "O.K., Dan. Thanks, John Akobe—I thought I'd had it that time! S-sorry I couldn't do anything about the packs, Dan."

He winced as Dan clapped him on a sore shoulder.

"Nobody's blaming you, old son! It was just one of those things! Now then, we'd better organize ourselves as soon as possible. We've still got our knives and one revolver—and we can make hammocks. G.B., you'd better take the revolver: John Akobe, what about the food and water situation?"

John Akobe covered the forest with a wave of his arm.

"We shall have enough."

"Right: we'll be depending on you for that. Now I

suggest we set to and make the hammocks. John Akobe, you and G.B. cut the lianas while Mike and I reconnoitre.''

Mike stamped his way to the back of the jetty. "It feels pretty solid. Do you think it really is a road, Dan?''

Six metres into the twilit forest Dan kicked a hole in the matted carpet of creepers, and poked with his knife.

"It's still stone underneath. Yes—I reckon it is.'' His eyes gleamed for a second. "The Incas almost certainly had a finger in it!''

They returned to the others, and within an hour the hammocks were complete. John Akobe cut four staves to help them along, and they were ready to set off again.

"I expect we'll find the growth comparatively light over the stone,'' said Dan. "Nothing could actually take root in the solid road—hence the Indian name, as we suspected. And we'll also have the benefit of Gregory's trail blazing!''

Mike judged the road to be about three metres wide, and almost straight. In places the ground had fallen away at one side, showing great blocks at least a man high and a metre more long. Dan walked fast, eagerly studying them.

"The Incas were hefty builders, weren't they!'' Mike remarked.

Dan was enthusiastic. "It's still a source of wonder how they fitted their great blocks so perfectly without using metal tools or mortar as we know it,'' he said. "There are traces of their roads and stone stairways all over their empire—from Quito to Argentina! We do know they had a pretty well-developed military system and government,'' he went on, "even if it was rather communistic! And you can't have either without good communications.''

"Didn't do them much good in the end—blow these flies!'' Mike remarked, swatting earnestly. "Probably used them for a quick getaway!''

"Not much sense in that,'' G.B. argued. "I would have

taken to the mountains, where foreigners—in armour at that—would be slowed up."

Dan smiled slightly. "Some did, of course. But it took quite a lot to slow up Pizarro and Co."

"Some did," Mike repeated thoughtfully. "The Spaniards didn't find Machu Picchu, did they? We know that for a fact."

Dan glanced at him sharply, then he smiled. "If you're thinking of the 'great ones' I don't imagine it's very likely. But I must admit, in this part of the world you never know!"

To Mike's relief the going for the first two days was relatively easy. Their worst troubles were the maddening, almost continual, buzz and prick of myriads of tiny flies, and the humid, stifling atmosphere.

The second evening there seemed no respite from the attacks of the insects, burrowing into every chink in their clothing, and attacking the heat- and damp-softened flesh.

Mike swatted desperately. "They're a sight worse than when we started!"

Dan and G.B. were in equal trouble. Only John Akobe was relativly unaffected by them.

"I should think we're near water," said Dan. "Another river or something."

"No river. Swamp." John Akobe raised his head and sniffed gently. "Swamp air."

Mike shook his head. "I can't smell anything unusual."

Dan laughed. "What John Akobe smells today, we smell tomorrow."

It was evening on the third day before they met the full force of the slimy black swamp ooze.

"Phew! I can smell it all right now!" Mike choked the frightful stench of rotten vegetation and fetid water out of his lungs. It hung heavy and stagnant in the humid air under the enclosing trees.

"Hurry—the air will clear soon," urged John Akobe,

and they lurched after him, stumbling and tripping over the clinging creepers.

Mike noticed the trees were becoming smaller, with masses of tangled roots sprawling over the ground like long gnarled fingers. The air was certainly less stagnant now that the trees were thinner overhead, but the smell still turned his inside.

"Getting slimy underfoot," Dan grunted. "Road must be sloping down."

Soon they were slithering and squelching at every step, and Dan called a halt.

"Looks to me as though the road goes right into it!" The ooze was obviously deeper on either side now. "Better go carefully."

A hundred metres further the trees ended, and Mike stared aghast.

A lake of desolate black water, a kilometre wide and twice as long, stretched across their path. Here and there a root stuck up in a weird hump, and vast patches of green slime lay perfectly still on the surface.

Mike glanced at John Akobe. He was standing just a little ahead sniffing the air.

"There certainly is an odd sort of smell," G.B. remarked, looking round, "apart from all the rest!"

"Anaconda," said John Akobe. Mike's scalp crept.

Dan gripped his staff. "Just the right place."

Mike saw it first: about ten metres to their right along the edge of the swamp, its long yellow-and-black splotched body coiled round a low branch.

"It's asleep," said John Akobe after a moment.

"But where there's one there's more." Dan frowned at the black water just beyond their feet, then up at a flight of geese whirring across the sky. "Two hours to dark—but we can't sleep here in this atmosphere." He poked forward into the black squelch. "Go carefully. Prod before you step and keep your eyes skinned."

Mike couldn't help a shudder as the opaque water

closed over his boots. Eyes and ears strained for any sign of the other anaconda, they moved slowly forward, making sure of the road just ahead with their staves before every step: but there was no other break in the water, save for the frequent "plip" of surfacing water-beetles.

All the way over Mike was conscious of the rumbling through the stones underfoot. Sometimes it was so strong as to shake the road and ripple the surface: at others it would die away to no more than a faint vibration.

Leg and nerve weary they squelched out at last, and not even the discomfort of his musty screwed-out clothes could keep Mike awake.

Crack of dawn found them on the march again.

They made good progress for the first three hours, then Mike noticed something peculiar.

"Am I seeing things, or are we going down?" He pointed his staff at the increasingly deep wall of creeper and roots on either side.

"No," said G.B.: "the forest is rising, I think. The base of the trees is higher every few yards."

"It looks like the beginning of an artificial cutting to me," said Dan; "dug on the level through the rising ground." He probed the creepers and sounded the wall with his staff. "Yes, listen: that's stone."

The great wall rose gradually on either side to a height of ten metres under a covering of moss and creeper. It reminded Mike of Winchester Cathedral—with the trees meeting in a green arch forty metres and more overhead. A crowd of monkeys swung across the treetops, at that distance so small he could hardly see them. The humid air hung heavy and oppressive.

An hour later the road itself began to rise, and the thick fleshy creepers of the low-lying wet forests changed for a thinner, drier kind. Soon the walls of stone blocks gave way to natural rock, and they were walking in a deep gorge the width of the road. The growth became less and less on the sides and overhead, letting the sun through in increasing strength. Their clothes began to steam in the heat.

Suddenly the walls ended—and Mike had never felt more insignificant.

They stood at the fork of two gorges, rising sheer to two hundred metres. The sun beat down mercilessly on dry bluish-brown rock. A startled brown lizard poised motionless on a stone, puffed out its throat at them, and darted away into a crack—the only living thing to be seen.

"Dried watercourse, I should imagine," said Dan. "Though I guess there was a natural crack to begin with. The road has followed the right fork, and now it apparently continues up the mainstream."

They turned into the mainstream, and as they walked Mike gazed up—and up—trying to see the awe-inspiring top of the towering sides. He saw more than that. Thousands of metres high in the brassy sky tiny specks were wheeling incessantly, never going beyond the lip of the gorge.

"Waiting for us, I expect!" Dan laughed, following Mike's gaze.

"They can wait!" Mike flapped his arms cheerfully. "I'd forgotten what it felt like to be dry all over! Not having a pack has its advantages, too—"

He stopped suddenly as he saw something ahead: something with a very familiar look, but gruesomely out of place outside the anatomy lecture room.

Mike ran forward, the others on his heels.

The gleaming white bones sprawled grotesquely in the bluish dust. The arms spread wide towards them over the head, and one knee bent awkwardly.

"They're certainly human," G.B. observed; "and recent."

"Too small for Gregory." Mike answered the query in every mind. "And the skull is the wrong shape for a European. More like an Indian."

"This armlet is Indian for sure," said Dan, touching the bronze band round the upper bone.

"What do you make of that?" G.B. pointed down into the rib cage.

Mike looked closely. "Third rib split underneath." He looked at Dan. "Does that mean what I think it means?"

"If you think it means he was stabbed in the back, I should say yes," said Dan grimly. "And judging by the gold armlet I should say he was the chief's first son. Gregory was never one to share profits."

"But—that's cold-blooded . . . !" Mike was horrified.

"So is explosive in a plane, and poisoned coffee!" said G.B. dryly.

Mike began to have a clearer idea of the nature of the "man with three fingers". . . .

"We can't bury him," Dan observed, looking round at the bare road. "We'll have to cover him with stones."

"How long do you reckon he's been here?" Mike laid the last stone and considered the neat cairn by the wall.

"Three days at least," said Dan. "It wouldn't take long with those fellas about—" they looked up at the wheeling black specks "—but it takes time to bleach bones to that extent."

"So he's picked up time somewhere," said Mike.

"It looks like it."

Their task finished, they moved on in silence, but Mike knew they were all thinking the same thing. If Gregory was still at least three days ahead they had no hope at all of getting to Xicchu first.

They rounded a curve in the road, and saw the mountains for the first time—rearing skyward, their rugged sides purple in the heat haze.

The heat in the gorge was unbearable: it was as dry and dusty as it had been humid before. In two hours of disheartened trudging and resting they saw nothing green, and no sign of life except a brittle-legged spider journeying down the sunbaked wall from one crack to another.

Mike rubbed the back of his hand on his britches and wiped the sweat from his eyes. The road sloped up fairly sharply now, but every few metres the gorge grew noticeably deeper. The sides seemed to sway in on him when he looked up. The great mountains loomed over them— huge unfriendly masses of immovable rock, reflecting the heat back into the gorge.

Mike wiped his eyes again: everything blurred and shimmered in front of him.

"Can't see anything yet, can you, G.B.?"

Mike rather admired him. From his taut, glistening face he was obviously still on his feet through sheer willpower alone.

"Lot more stones about!" Mike remarked after a few minutes. "Ground's getting thick with them." He found the energy to kick one. "Rumbling is nearer, as well, isn't it?"

The rumbling, apparently from directly underneath, vibrated through the soles of his feet.

Suddenly he stood still, the back of his neck pricking. "What the dickens was that!"

They all stood and stared at one another as a disembodied wail flowed round them, echoing from wall to wall along the gorge, and dying out behind them.

Dan let out his breath and chuckled.

"It was a horn of some kind! Their lookout must have spotted us." His mouth tightened again. "Well, we'll soon know if Gregory has prepared the ground for us or not. They apparently received Keith well, and the odds are they'll treat us likewise, but. . . ."

"But it all depends on Gregory!" Mike finished for him. "Though I should think it pretty likely he assumes we've been stopped by one of his booby traps," he added optimistically.

"We'll soon know!" G.B. was the first to see the great boulder blocking their way as they rounded another curve in the road.

"Watch your step," Dan warned.

54

They advanced steadily.

Mike glanced back at the sheer sides of the gorge and the complete absence of cover behind them.

"Better put a good face on it," he remarked, "we couldn't get away if we wanted to!"

"So this is the growling mountain...." G.B. looked up. "Mind your heads!"

A shower of small stones rattled down the mountainside, bouncing and spinning, to scatter themselves over the road ahead.

"The vibration must have dislodged them," said Dan. "Keep a lookout for anything bigger."

They approached the "road block" firmly, but warily. Dan grunted under his breath. "Ah—I thought so: here's the reception committee."

Mike stiffened, ready for trouble. He realized he'd been working up to it for the last hour or more. But evidently it wasn't coming yet.

The two men who appeared round the boulder were certainly Indians, but taller and broader than the Marubi: light brown, with long, straight black hair and a short fringe, and an even stronger hint of the Mongolian in their broad faces and high cheekbones. Their plain brown tunic struck a dim chord with Mike, as did the deep round collar-cum-breastplate, apparently of bronze. Their bronze knife and spear looked businesslike, but their attitude, though alert, was clearly not hostile. They approached silently on soft sandals, their slightly almond-shaped black eyes questioning.

"Wait here," Dan ordered, and went forward to meet them. He held up his hand in salute, and spoke in Quechua.

"Greetings, men of Xicchu. We come in peace seeking the great one who rules in the growling mountain."

The Indians exchanged a glance, then one, without a word but somehow conveying courtesy, lifted his spear in the direction of the boulder.

"So far, so good," Dan muttered as they passed in single file between the boulder and the sheer rock face. "They understood my version of Quechua, anyway. It's like talking school Latin to an ancient Roman, I should imagine! I guess we have Keith's standing to thank for the lack of opposition," he added. "Let's hope Gregory doesn't spoil their impression of white men too soon!"

The gorge still curved away in front of them: before long they were actually walking in a cleft in the moutain.

"What did you make of them?" said G.B.

"It looks as though Mike's idea was nearer the mark than I thought," said Dan.

Mike glanced at him quickly, but Dan was quite serious.

"You mean—they're Incas?" G.B.'s eyebrows lifted. "A lost tribe, as it were?"

Dan smiled. "That's rather a romantic way of putting it but they're certainly a 'superior' people of the Inca type."

Four high-pitched notes wailed past them, echoing on up the gorge.

"One each," Mike observed. "Their lookout system is well organized anyway. But I thought the present-day Incas were rather, well, degraded, and so on."

"So they are, pitifully so. But if these people are isolated enough to have avoided outside influences, they may have developed along their own lines. It's a pure guess, of course, but from what we've seen of the terrain on this side, I should say it's possible—which is more than I'd have said a few weeks ago!"

Mike strained his eyes up at the bare rock.

"You mean they may be living as the Incas did?"

"Not exactly. A people almost always either goes forward or degenerates. But they may have kept some of the ancient culture and ways. Their whole system and empire was completely founded on sun worship, if you remember."

"Ugh!" said Mike, with feeling.

Dan chuckled. "From the look on your face I should think you're getting mixed up with the Aztecs! The Incas weren't as bad as those boys—fairly quiet on the whole, I'd say. Peaceful, and very keen on acting and singing, etcetera. We gather they had a song or dance for most occasions! But, of course, there's no knowing which way they've developed."

Mike looked up at the narrow strip of sky now over a thousand metres above them—and found himself shuddering. Perhaps it was the hard, lowering rock, but there was something oppressive in the air. Probably the famous "unfriendliness of the Andes". Dan seemed to notice it, too, and followed Mike's glance.

"A shower from that height could do quite a bit of damage, couldn't it?" he remarked thoughtfully. "They're pretty safe from this side anyway."

"That was one of the Inca defence tactics, wasn't it?" said G.B.

For a while they trudged on in silence, and Mike tried to remember everything he knew about the Incas, just in case.

"Hope we're out of this before dark," G.B. said at last. "I don't fancy having to spend the night in this crack in the earth's skin!"

Mike secretly agreed. He'd never have admitted it aloud, but he was getting the creeps. He was no more sensitive to atmosphere than anyone else of his type— but there was something grim about this place. He looked up again at the blank, unfeeling rock towering over them.

It was completely contemptuous of their very existence. . . .

5

POWER POLITICS

But for the next hour Mike hadn't the breath to think of atmosphere.

"Phew! How long do you think this will go on for, Dan?" he grunted. "The gradient must be 1-in-1 I should think! I'll bet the Incas didn't have a song for this—they wouldn't have had the puff!"

Dan grinned. "Bear up, Mike: there's no knowing! This part of the world suffered a terrific upheaval at one time—when all these peaks and ravines came about."

"I shouldn't think the outpost would be too far from base," G.B. panted. "They didn't seem to have any home comforts for a long stay, did they?"

"Might know a short cut!" said Mike.

"There's one good thing," said Dan: "the higher we go the cooler it will get. Though let's hope we don't have to climb as far as the snow line! If there is any connection with the old Incas, though, they built pretty high in places. And there's another thing fairly certain: we won't see anything until we're right on top of it."

"Like Machu Picchu." Mike remembered his first sight of the ancient city, high up on its own island of rock and forest, so inaccessible it had been lost for all those generations.

With shocking suddenness the road ended—in a sheer drop of two or three hundred metres.

"I say—that's a bit risky!" G.B. breathed. "These lads want a few hints on safety first!"

Mike gazed down into the V-shaped ravine, his nerves tingling. He could see this great slice of the earth slipping down, heeling over and away as the molten rocks heaved and subsided beneath it. Now a silver thread of river showed at the bottom, and the steep sides were thick with green growth. It was an almost unbelievable relief to see this sign of life at last.

"Where do we go from here, Dan?" Mike asked cheerfully—and quickly sobered when Dan pointed to a narrow path along the edge of the ravine and round the spur of rock to their right. "But we can't walk along that!"

Dan grinned at him slyly.

"Thought you'd be glad of the experience: it's a typical Inca path!"

The path led back to a broad shelf of grass- and bush-covered rock on the other side of the spur.

Dan's breath hissed—and no one spoke for a long moment.

"Machu Picchu again," said Mike at last.

Across a hundred metres wide ravine hung a "rope" bridge. Beyond, backed by mountain, the Indian city straggled up an out-cropping of rock, drab grey and stolid. Below it—in front of them and to the left—the rock sloped down steeply to the fork of the river at the bottom of the ravine, in a series of man-made brown earth terraces, which Mike recognized at once as obviously Inca.

Beyond the little rectangular stone buildings across the ravine were peaks, and more peaks: some stark and rugged, and topped with snow, some lush green. But Mike was more consciously impressed by the grim backcloth to the city—a bleak, bare face of rock, dwarfing the grey houses that crept up between its feet.

"Impressive, in a grim sort of way," G.B. remarked, and Mike brought his gaze back with a jerk from the thousand metre level. "Though stone blocks of that size aren't my idea of building material!"

"When you see their temple and the ruler's 'palace', if they've got one, you may change your mind," said Dan. "The Incas were some of the finest builders ever—wonderful lines——"

Mike pounced on Dan's admission. "You think it really is Inca then?"

"Maybe." Dan smiled. "But our first job is to establish contact! The only way seems to be over the rope bridge: and as they're probably watching us anyway it wouldn't add to our prestige to try to hide ourselves. We could wait till dark, but I don't think it would help us at all in the long run."

Dan tried the bridge, and took a few tentative steps along it.

"Wait a minute!" G.B. hung back. "They've only got to cut the bridge when we're all on it."

Dan moved forward carefully. "They won't. The Incas had a curiously strong taboo about destroying bridges."

Mike agreed with that: it was one of the acknowledged reasons why the Spaniards had made such speedy progress.

Mike followed Dan. Once he was used to the sagging sway of the bridge he risked another look at the city. It was quite big really—a couple of thousand people, he estimated—with closely packed thatched houses climbing on terraces to more than a hundred metres up the mountain. He couldn't see the lower level for the stone wall all round. His heart began to beat a little fast with a not unpleasant anticipation.

He heard the singing with a mixture of surprise and—he wouldn't have admitted it—relief, almost before they stepped on to firm ground again.

"This is it!" Dan grunted. "But I think we're all right: that doesn't sound like a war song."

Mike had gathered that the Incas were fond of bright colours, and apparently these people had inherited the leaning! The crowd, beginning to flow through the opening in the wall, livened the place up no end, he thought. He felt a bit of a fool standing there on the grass being sung to, so did G.B. apparently, but Dan and John Akobe took it all in their stride.

At last a young Indian, whom Mike marked out as someone of some standing, came forward and addressed Dan. Mike couldn't catch all the words, but the meaning was obvious. Mike liked his lean hardness, and his straight look; and he carried his waving scarlet and white feathers like an Indian chief—which, Mike reflected, he probably was! A bit young, though: not much older than himself. But he wore the three-tiered belt on his white tunic— more than likely he was the chief's son.

Mike was none too sorry to follow Dan's lead and sit down on the litter held for him by two broad-backed Indians in blue tunics. If the streets were mostly stairways, like Machu Picchu, he'd be glad of the ride: he'd done enough climbing for one day! Surrounded by the childishly excited—and incongruously well built!— crowd, they took the "main street": a broad stairway leading up from the city gate. Other narrow stairways on either side led off and up between Eastern-style compounds, many with the garden on the next terrace behind, on a level with the thatched roof. So far they were certainly true to type.

The crowd seemed much less actually curious about them than Mike expected. Then he remembered: they weren't the first white men they'd seen. Keith was here somewhere. Mike frowned. Just where was Keith? And Gregory? His complacency shrivelled suddenly.

The procession crossed a broad paved square. Mike studied the high, almost white building to their right, apparently backing into the mountain. Probably the temple: it was massive enough. First-rate stonework, though—even G.B. couldn't complain; great stones fitting into one another with hardly a crack. Dan was right: wonderful lines. Ah, this one was probably the "palace".

Impressive in its way, like everything else. Smallish, but solid.

Mike relaxed a little as they "dismounted" on the broad grey steps. Oh well, Dan seemed fairly happy for the moment, and there was no point in meeting trouble half-way: though Mike knew none of them would be really easy until they knew what Gregory was up to. And perhaps then less than ever! But for the present they were popular and welcome guests, being conducted with speed and courtesy to the guest rooms.

Mike stood and surveyed his allotted quarters. Pretty bare except for some blue and red hangings and a bed built out sideways from the wall. And he could see no possible use for the enormous pottery vase at the foot of the bed—it must have been nearly two metres high!

The bed didn't look too soft either. He winced as he pressed it. Solid grey stone under a pile of red blankets! Otherwise all mod. cons.—if a jet of cold spring water from a spout in the wall constituted a mod. con.! But it was good to have a really clean sluice down. It occurred to him that the vase might be a kind of bath, but he decided not to try it. There'd be a powerful element of risk in getting out again!

Dan was finishing a crude shave when Mike looked in on him eventually.

"They only have tweezers it seems," he explained with a wry grin. "So Keith's 'valet' brought me his razor."

Mike pounced again. "Where is he, Dan?"

"Investigating some burial caves in the mountains. He's all right so far: has a pretty good name, needless to say." Dan's smile faded quickly. "But Gregory's with him, I gather."

"So Keith can't know who he really is."

"That's not surprising. I'm rather curious myself as to what he really looks like." He rinsed the razor thoughtfully. "What an actor that man would have made. I wonder what tale he told to account for his being here.

It would have to be pretty convincing to get past Keith."

"I wonder—"

But Mike's wonderings were interrupted by a welcome summons to eat.

They sat on the floor and dipped with a will into shallow brightly coloured dishes.

"Not much sign of the Incas' fabulous wealth here!" G.B. remarked, when the soft-treading servants had left them alone at last.

Mike took in the almost bare room, like his own on a large scale, and agreed.

"These Indians must have terrifically strong muscles!" he groaned. "I prefer a back to my heap of blankets! I say—talking of backs—did you notice that little feller's hand? Keith's valet."

"I noticed it wasn't there—if that's what you mean!" G.B. grunted.

"Neat job, wasn't it!" Mike was professionally enthusiastic. "Must have come off with one—" He caught Dan's eye. "All right, Dan, sorry! Not during meals!"

Then John Akobe spoke for the first time in Mike's hearing since their arrival in the city.

"Keith," he said.

A moment later Mike, too, heard the sound of boots on stone, and a dishevelled, hard-breathing Keith Oban gusted through the doorway. He looked just the same as Mike remembered him: perhaps a shade leaner and more tanned. He stood still for a long moment, running long fingers through his dark hair, his lively brown eyes screwed up in a mixture of amazement and laughter.

"Well, well. Welcome to Xicchu!" he murmured quizzically at last. "Are you going to tell me, or do I have to guess?"

He sat on the floor, his eyes fixed on Dan, while the latter told their story. He smiled wryly when Dan finished.

"So I've just spent three days alone in the mountains with Matthew Gregory himself!" he said softly. "No wonder he was so keen to stick to me! Thought I might give something away about the 'light', I suppose. I'm afraid he won't get far in that direction, though."

"You'll have to put us in the picture, Keith," said Dan. "We're starting from absolute scratch as far as this place is concerned."

Keith glanced at his watch. "According to custom they'll expect you at sunset. It's a long tale, but you'd better have it all—there's just about time. When you come here," he said, exchanging a glance with John Akobe, "you have to forget absolutely everything you've always taken for granted—in modes of thought, outlook, and so on, I mean, as well as civilization as we know it. You have to try and grasp the completely primitive mind of these people—and the particular kind of intolerance which goes with it." He paused and glanced at Dan. "You've gathered, of course, they're a kind of offshoot of the Incas. Whether they're descended directly from them I wouldn't like to say, but all things considered I'd say it's reasonably likely." Keith chuckled. "They're as proud as possible of their ancestry, and say their line of rulers goes back direct to Huascar."

Dan's eyebrows rose. "The last legal Inca."

Mike nodded. "Huascar—assassinated by Atahualpa, who was executed by Pizarro—and so on! Wasn't that it?"

"That was it. The name is perpetuated in each ruler. There's still no writing, and I can't get the hang of the quipus yet, but I gather all their traditions and history are still preserved on them."

Mike caught a sideways look from G.B. "System of knotted strings for keeping records and things," he muttered.

"And now we come to the fly in the treacle tin," Keith went on. "The succession. And this is where their simple minds show up. I don't mean it in a derogatory sense at all: 'childlike' might be a better description. You may have noticed something of it in their welcome. They're like all really primitive people—" he smiled slightly "—even European ones: they're carried away by 'signs and wonders', and anything with a supernatural touch." He raised an eyegrow at Dan. "You remember how the first Inca obtained his standing? I think it's relevant—and typical of the kind of thing that impresses them."

"You mean, as Child of the Sun?" Dan smiled. "A shrewd piece of showmanship, if we're both thinking of the same story."

"What happened?" Mike hadn't heard this.

"They made him a tunic covered in plates of gold," said Dan; "they had plenty in those days, as you know. And they arranged for him to nip out of a cave on the mountainside at the precise moment the sun struck the place at the proper angle. The people down below, of course, had been primed, and saw what they had been led to expect."

"The sun apparently standing on the mountain in the shape of a man," said G.B. "Hm.—I can see the effect that would have." He shot a quick look at Dan. "Is that true?"

"So far as we know." Dan was perfectly serious. "It's the same trick that's still being played by power-hunters on credulous people—from confidence tricksters to African witch doctors. The principle's the same the world over, and always has been. It's amazing how people will be bowled over by a flashy display, without trying to work out what's behind it."

Mike began to see the relevance Keith had mentioned. "And that's where the 'light' comes in?" he suggested.

"Exactly," said Keith. "They still worship the sun—" he hesitated slightly "—for the most part. The fragment I sent you was the size of a small pea. I understand the whole lump is as big as a man's head. You know how that fragment shone: I think we can just about imagine what the other would be like!"

Mike remembered the blinding glare in the lab., and G.B. spoke his thoughts.

"It would look like the sun itself."

"And the succession hinges on the possession of it," Keith finished. "The man who holds the sun in his hands has always been the absolutely undisputed ruler—Child of the Sun."

"And the people swallow it, I suppose," said Dan. "They would, of course." He frowned. "Though I would have thought its lethal aspect would carry considerable weight as well!"

"Not as much as one might expect. The only time it was tried it produced a rather curious result. That particular property was discovered by an unfortunate accident, of course——"

"I should imagine there were a number of unfortunate accidents until they learned how to insulate it," said Dan grimly.

Keith assented. "One or two. But don't forget that to them there's no such thing as a physical property. If anything harms it's because of the intelligence behind it —its spirit or devil."

Mike began to feel that his mental gymnastics were producing results. He was really beginning to understand something of how these people looked at things.

"One of the earlier Huascars was something of an opportunist by all accounts," Keith went on. "He tried to strengthen his position in the obvious way—but he had an 'unfortunate accident' himself!"

"And they took it that the spirit behind the 'light' was angry with him," Dan finished.

"Exactly. It hasn't been tried since. The spirit of——"

At that moment the little one-handed servant appeared in the doorway and caught Keith's eye.

Keith got up. "Time to go." And Mike realized with a jolt of surprise that the daylight had nearly disappeared.

The "palace" hummed with activity. Soft-footed Indians passed in and out of doorways, and brushed by them in the lamp-lit stone corridors. It looked to Mike as though someone were keeping them on their toes.

"That will be Tupac," Keith smiled when Mike mentioned it. "The laddie who met you—Huascar's son. Bit of a live wire!"

Mike tried to see in the door ways as they passed, but most had heavy blue wool curtains drawn across. He was no judge of materials, but the curtains looked like good stuff. As G.B. had remarked, there was no sign of the legendary wealth of the Incas. Well, he hadn't really expected there would be : but what they had was obviously good work. That was one tradition they'd kept up, anyway. The lamps intrigued him, too: floating wicks in shallow dishes gave a pleasant, if dim, amber light from niches along the walls.

They passed between brown-clad guards, like those they had first met, into the lamp-lit "throne room"—and Mike was suddenly very conscious of his own scruffy appearance.

The big, austere room seemed full of feathers—scarlet and iridescent green, purple and gold, like a flock of humming birds—waving from heads and ears and knees and trying to outglow the vivid tunics and cloaks which rippled and swayed in a continuous eye-confusing movement. Slanting black eyes watched them as they walked the length of the room.

Even Mike couldn't help being impressed by the real dignity of the tall, broad-faced Indian who rose to greet them from the stone couch at the far end of the room.

So this was Huascar, descendant of the Great Inca, Child of the Sun!

The scarlet and white plumes on his mitre-like bronze headdress, and his scarlet and white cloak and tunic, all added up to near majesty. But Mike's eyes were held by the short red fringe fastened to the front of the headdress, and falling over Huascar's broad forehead. It was the llauta—the sacred fringe of the Incas! They might almost have been looking at the Great Inca himself.

Mike was soon left well behind in the rapid exchange of

Quechua between Huascar and Keith. His attention slipped to the other figures on either side of Huascar. One was the young Indian who had met them—Tupac, wasn't it? That was an old Inca name, too, if Mike remembered rightly. Tupac caught Mike's eye, and his mouth twitched slightly. Mike confirmed his first impressions to himself: likeable type—he wouldn't mind seeing a bit more of him.

But who was the chap on the other side, with the beak of a nose? Mike probed his memory: long sober grey robe and cloak, and plain silver semicircular headdress thing. Now what did that mean? Narrowed black eyes were scrutinizing them one by one. Mike tried to stare him out —the chap put his back up! They were hard, shrewd eyes. Yet there was an unmistakable likeness to Huascar —could almost be a relation.... Mike's memory came up to scratch. The High Priest—that was it! That grey was the official undress uniform, and, of course, he would actually be a brother or uncle of the ruler. But he was a different type altogether—and Mike guessed he didn't like playing second fiddle! He was probably behind the trouble that Keith had half implied.

Talking of trouble, he'd forgotten Gregory in all this! No, there was no sign of him. Well, he'd probably lie low now they'd all arrived. He must know by this time, surely. And if Huascar could be convinced about him they'd have him cornered, and on his own. Unless.... Mike's glance slid back to the High Priest.

But the formalities were over.

"Keith's asked him for a private audience," Dan murmured in his ear. "We've got to warn him about Gregory."

The room emptied rapidly at Huascar's gesture. He listened gravely to their story, while the younger man's piercing look flashed between Keith and Dan. He could hardly wait for Dan to finish.

"Give me leave, my father—I will kill this dog who

eats our meat and deceives us!" The bronze blade of his knife glinted in the flickering lamplight.

Mike was glad he wasn't on the receiving end of the look Huascar shot at his son.

"Have you forgotten the Law so soon, my son!"

Tupac suddenly subsided, apparently squashed, though Mike guessed it wouldn't last long. But Huascar hadn't finished yet. "Illa Tici Vira-Cocha requires that a man be master of himself," he said severely, and Tupac's face darkened with a flush of genuine shame.

"The Law must be obeyed at whatever cost." There was firm decision in every line of Huascar's face as he continued: "This evil man shall be found—"

He stopped suddenly.

"And—?"

The High Priest stood in a narrow doorway to their left.

Mike wasn't used to the ways of primitive courts, but even he could see the man had a nerve to butt in like that!

Huascar recovered himself at once.

"What have you to say, High Priest of Xicchu?" His cool dignity would have withered anyone else.

"Just this, Huascar." Mike winced at the tone. "The white man eats from my dish and drinks from my jar. Let him who touches him take care to himself!"

The twinge of apprehension Mike had felt earlier came back with a rush when he caught the look on Keith's face. This was a battle for personal power—and something bigger than Mike knew hung on the outcome.

Huascar's calm was unbroken.

"I rule in this city, Huaman." It was a quiet statement of unarguable fact.

The High Priest's lip lifted slightly.

"While you live, Huascar."

"Which shall be as long as Vira-Cocha pleases."

The High Priest stood for a moment regarding Huascar with amused and obvious contempt. Then, with what

Mike could only describe as a "mocking bow", he went out, taking his time.

Tupac stood watching his father eagerly, his brown fingers gripping the hilt of his knife.

But Huascar had forgotten them all. He stared anxiously into infinite distances beyond them. Mike tried to understand Keith's expression, too. Nothing he could think of would call for this reaction. And Keith was deeper in it—whatever it was!—than any of them had realized.

It was queer: Mike had always been inclined to look on anyone who wasn't English, or at least white, as not being quite the same as he; without feelings or something, he'd never analysed it. But now it was different somehow. Here were these insignificant brown people, and Keith was putting himself right alongside them. Mike glanced at Huascar and Tupac. Their faces glowed bronze in the lamplight, but the differing emotions on them were universal.

When it came to emotion Mike tended to flounder a bit. He shifted and looked at Dan, who seemed to feel as superfluous as he did himself.

Dan quickly organized a strategic withdrawal, and they gathered in his room to await Keith.

"Looks like a rift in the domestic lute," G.B. observed.

"But none of them expected it," said Mike, "judging by the looks on their faces."

Dan considered the lamp in the wall niche.

"I think you're wrong there, Mike: I'd say they expected it all right, but not so soon or so openly."

G.B. sat in the window opening and studied his nails with exaggerated interest.

"May I take it you have forgotten our concern is with Gregory?" he said coolly. "I must acknowledge I personally have very little interest in the political affairs of obscure savages," he added.

"Then you'd better find some," said Dan with deceptive evenness; "because if I'm not mistaken Gregory is in them up to the neck." G.B. glared at Dan, but Dan had dismissed him already. "I would guess the High Priest had had an unexpected boost," he went on.

Mike raised his eyebrows. "Gregory?"

"Gregory." He was answered from the doorway.

A grave Keith joined him on the edge of Dan's "bed".

"Things have come to flash-point sooner than we expected," he said soberly. "We had hoped to avoid it until we could find a way out."

"But why doesn't Huascar just clap the High Priest in irons—or whatever they do in these parts?" Mike argued. "Huascar's the ruler, after all!"

Keith smiled slightly. "It's not quite so simple as that, I'm afraid. Despite all we said just now, Huascar's position isn't quite as secure as it looks. As I mentioned before, there's a snag in it. The ruler has always—and only—held his authority by possession of the 'light', the 'light' apparently being contained in a ceremonial mask known as the Head of Huascar: and there is the belief that if it isn't treated with due respect the spirit of the original Huascar will take vengeance. The episode I described confirmed that belief, of course. But nowadays it's sometimes touch and go between the people's fear of the wrath of the spirit of Huascar, which they haven't experienced, and the more concrete wrath of their wretched god—as conveyed by the High Priest, of course."

"What's this other god?" said Dan. "Don't they worship the sun now?"

"Indirectly, yes: Xicchu is their symbol."

"This is all something new for Incas, isn't it?" G. B. broke in.

"Not in principle. These things evolve into different forms of expression. And we have to remember they're a good three to four hundred years from their original situation, even as we know of it."

Mike's brain had been ticking over, and now he came to his conclusions.

"So it would be a good thing for the High Priest if he could undermine the prestige of the 'light'."

Keith paused a moment before replying. "It would be an even better thing if the ruler were to die without passing on the knowledge of the hiding-place to his heir."

Mike gaped at him.

"Is that how it's done? My hat—that's a bit risky, isn't it? It's a wonder the line has lasted so long."

Keith smiled. "They're pretty shrewd about it!"

"Still it could happen! But if that would give the High Priest a good chance, why has the authority of the 'light' itself lasted so long—if it hasn't been 'used'?"

"We have to take into consideration that the High Priest himself has always believed in it as well," said Dan; "though our friend Huaman seems a bit sceptical, I'll admit!"

"Exactly," said Keith. "And a few well-chosen words of encouragement were all he needed."

Mike hissed between his teeth. "And Gregory was just the one to give them!"

"Exactly," said Keith again. "The scepticism may have been there before from time to time, but it had no backing and fizzled out. Scepticism, as well as faith, needs to be fed."

"But the force really is there if the ruler wants to use it to keep his position," Mike argued.

"Quite: but don't forget to them it has a mind of its own," said Keith. "They're not going to risk offending it again. From their point of view it's a big chance to take—'While there's life there's hope', and so forth!"

"I suppose so." Mike had to agree.

Dan regarded Keith shrewdly.

"And if it came to it, would the High Priest take over —just like that? Without any opposition? Although I admit five or six hundred years of the Inca system wouldn't make for initiative among the people."

Keith didn't answer for a moment, and Mike caught a swift meaning glance between him and the statue-like John Akobe. The flickering lamp cast deep shadows round Keith's eyes, and made curious lines on his face. Mike suddenly felt that stupid breath of fear that had made his heart race before.

"No, there wouldn't be any opposition, if you mean any kind of civil war," said Keith at last. "The people would believe that the spirit of Huascar had rejected the line in favour of the High Priest, and their superstition would bind them just as firmly under him. He'd see to that. But...." He broke off. "Who served you when you arrived?" he asked.

"Served us?" said Dan. "One of the Indians—your servant, I gather. Small, cheerful sort of man. One hand. Why?"

"He was one of the first in the city to commit himself to follow Christ—or as they call Him, Vira-Cocha."

G.B. looked up sharply, and Mike had a sudden sick feeling that he knew what Keith was going to say—and he didn't want to hear it.

6

MIKE TRIES TO REMEMBER

But Keith said it.

"It has already cost him that hand."

Mike's throat dried up. Something he'd always secretly dreaded facing was suddenly dangling in front of him before he'd had a chance to put up his guard. Something he'd never told anybody about. He'd taken the usual leg-pulling about what he believed in, of course, and even learned to ride the meaner sneers: but he'd always been scared that if he had to meet any solid persecution he'd put on a pretty poor front. He knew it had happened right enough in the early days—but second-century Rome was a long while ago! Then there had been China—and Middle Europe. It still happened. But as far as Mike was concerned, only in the papers—and a safe way off.

And now, within the last hour, he had actually spoken to a man to whom it had happened. Here in this little city, barely a kilometre square—and cut off from the rest of the world.

"H-how?" The word forced its way out at last.

Keith shrugged. "He raised a disrespectful fist to the temple. A couple of priests relieved him of it." The hardness in Keith's eyes cancelled his easy tone.

"And no one did anything about it," said Dan. It was a statement rather than a question.

"Just so," said Keith.

Mike almost squeaked. "Do you mean to say they got away with it!"

Mike was suddenly out of his depth. He hadn't thought twice about chasing after Gregory—fighting something he could see and touch, more or less—but now, without warning, they'd taken a header into the deep end.

Keith smiled slightly. "Not altogether. Huascar had plenty to say about it. But there was nothing he could do. The whole system is too powerful; and perhaps he hadn't the courage then." He looked at Dan. "I think you can get an idea from that sample why it's absolutely essential the High Priest doesn't get a real hold. There will be more than hands lost if his filthy Xicchu raises its vile head in earnest."

"You mean there'd be a fast trip downhill?"

"If Huaman gained absolute power he'd use mighty strong means to keep it absolute." Keith smiled slightly. "He has the people's mentality pretty shrewdly summed up—much more so than Huascar has. He knows how to impress them. He has been doing his best now for a long time, and got as far as sacrificing a macaw—with the appropriate trimmings—but Huascar came down on him like a ton of bricks."

"Do we take it that Huascar is committed as well?" said Dan.

Keith nodded. "And Tupac. Huaman realizes that in those two is his strongest centre of opposition: and there are about twenty other known Christians in the city. He knows they'd be a menace to the kind of power he wants."

The water grew deeper as Mike looked at it. Keith went on.

"He had carefully cultivated and built on the superstitions of nearly a thousand years, and the conversion of Huascar put a time-bomb in his very foundations."

"Which from his point of view has to be defused before it has a chance to go off," said Dan. He pursed his lips thoughtfully. "And, as you say, the ideal way would be for Huascar to die without passing on the information re the Head of Huascar."

"That's why we're keeping a private twenty-four hour watch on him. He can't, or won't, recognize the situation for what it is."

"You can't do that for ever!" G.B. observed suddenly. "And I don't really see that it concerns us who has the upper hand! In any case it would be all the better for us if the thing were lost." He shrugged sarcastically. "Though, of course, the fact that we came out to stop Gregory getting hold of it doesn't seem to matter any longer!"

"You realize, of course," said Dan smoothly, "that if Huaman gets the 'upper hand' there'll almost certainly be no end to the damage in this place—beginning with that twenty, and carrying on with any more who step out of line."

The spark was crackling once more.

G.B. shrugged again. "Even granted the High Priest is a nasty piece of work, I really don't see there'd be all that harm done. Oh, I know cutting off hands and so on sounds grim to us, but they're only primitive people, after all."

"A primitive hand is still a hand to its loser!"

Mike butted in. Perhaps after all Dan was rather exaggerating things.

"But it surely couldn't be as bad as all that, could it, Keith? I mean, they're fairly civilized in their own way, aren't they?"

Keith considered him for a moment: then he got up. "You might as well judge for yourselves."

Mike told himself not to be an ass as they crossed the now empty moonlit square; most places look unfriendly in the moonlight. It was just the cold light on the grey stone, with no one about. That was all.

The temple was much bigger than Mike had thought. Its flat front towered over them, the white moonlight giving it a certain smooth, hard beauty. Its far end was lost in the jagged black shadows under the mountain.

Keith hesitated for a second on the broad top step,

then led the way under the massive single stone lintel.

Mike couldn't see a thing at first. Then his eyes gradually picked up the amber glow from flickering lamps in niches along the apparently bare walls, a good way away on either side of them. He probed the shadows ahead without result as Keith led them in deeper. There was no sound except their footsteps echoing in emptiness. Mike caught a queer, sweetish smell from somewhere, but couldn't put a name to it. Herbs, or something.

Then Keith's faintly ironic voice came quietly across the darkness.

"There he is—the mighty Xicchu."

Mike's heart thumped a little as he peered forward. He couldn't see anything at first except the glow of three or four lamps on a shelf about four metres ahead. Then his eyes caught a dull gleam of something else behind them, and followed it upward.

Writhing up from a thick coil, its scaly body winking bronze in the yellow light, was a great serpent.

Mike didn't think he was any more imaginative than most, but as he gazed up at the top-heavy, spade-shaped head hanging high over them, he felt an unreasoning flash of fear. The deep red eyes reflected the flickering lamps with an almost hypnotic realism in the dimness. But underneath what Mike quickly recognized as clever psychological showmanship was a current of evil—beastly, powerful evil. The kind of evil he knew is still sometimes stumbled on in primitive places—the kind of evil that grips the instincts and emotions until they override all reasoned thinking and human decency—and that gives a fearful power to the man who is strong enough to direct the results.

Mike began to understand. So, apparently, did the others: even G.B. seemed subdued.

"Go on, Keith," said Dan after a moment.

Keith led the way up four broad, shallow steps, and Mike found himself looking down on what he had thought was a shelf at the foot of the serpent. It was a large stone block.

Mike tingled. He'd seen one of these before. He sized it up—three metres, by about two, and one high. He ran his fingers over the top in a sober excitement. Yes—it was rough in the middle just the same.

"Machu Picchu," he exclaimed. "It's the same as the block there, Dan. Flaked off in the same way."

That particular mystery had always intrigued Mike, as it had experienced archaeologists: the solid granite altar flaked on the top by what was acknowledged to have been an extraordinarily intense heat. And here was another similar—in actual use.

"You're right of course, Mike." Dan was studying one of two pairs of bronze rings about three metres apart towards either end of the block. "Though these are an extra. Haven't been used for some time, I should say. Must have been put there for a purpose in the first place, though," he added thoughtfully.

Mike suddenly withdrew his hand. That was a possibility he hadn't thought of. He shook it off impatiently. That was going too far! The Incas didn't make that kind of sacrifice—often. . . .

"Any theories about the heat source, Keith?" said Dan.

"No theories needed. Look up there."

Keith took two of the lamps and held them up at arm's length. Directly above them hung a large, roughly oval lump of some translucent substance, suspended, presumably, from the unseen roof.

"It's surely not glass!" Dan exclaimed.

"Rock crystal. Ground to a powerful lens. The thatch is removed every morning, and it focuses the sun all day."

"And reaches its hottest over the block. I see." Dan nodded. "If it's a strong lens I guess it could account for the flaking all right—and for anything else that got in its way!"

Keith replaced the lamps. "Well, there you are. I need hardly say that if Huascar goes under, this—" he gestured sharply "—will be in commission again within a month."

Dan's eyes narrowed. "Do you really think so? I know such sacrifices weren't altogether unknown, but would he go that far, even against the Christians?" He smiled faintly. "Though I imagine the psychological effect would be pretty powerful!"

"I'm quite sure he would if they got in his way. He'd have a strong precedent, wouldn't he?"

Mike had forgotten the two Spanish monks in the early days. The method had been different—though still pretty rotten—but the result was the same.

"The wise hunter knows, when warrior ants march nothing but fire will turn them from their chosen path," John Akobe quoted in his quiet way.

Keith smiled in the dimness. "By the grace of God, in this case not even fire," he said softly.

"Let's get out of here!" said G.B. suddenly, and so loudly that Mike jumped. So the atmosphere was even getting G.B. down: the cool, rational G.B.! As they made their way back Mike glanced at him—and was puzzled.

There was positive fear on G.B.'s face.

But when they emerged into the moonlit square the expression had gone. Mike took long breaths of cool, clean air—clean, he felt, in more ways than one.

"Well, I think we have a reasonably clear idea of the sort of thing that will be let loose if Xicchu takes over," said Dan after a silent few moments' walking towards the palace. "Personally, I think we're morally bound to do our best to stop it."

"I think we're nothing of the kind!"

Everyone looked at G.B. His face was pale and tight, and angry.

"I still say our only concern is with Gregory and the 'light'. The politics and religious squabbles of a tribe of

Indians are nothing to do with us. And in any case, the question doesn't arise!" he snapped.

Dan considered G.B. levelly for a moment.

"Perhaps you're right there," he said dryly. "The question doesn't arise—yet."

"I say, that's the one-handed laddie coming at us, isn't it?" Mike exclaimed.

The little Indian, almost incoherent in his agitation, rushed down the palace steps and grabbed Keith's arm with his good hand.

"Huascar—quickly—very ill!" he gasped.

Mike's ears pricked. He glanced swiftly at Dan and received a nod.

He presented his credentials in jerks as he ran with Keith back into the palace.

Mike could see there was something very wrong with Huascar. His face and chest were damp with sweat, and he seemed to have great difficulty in breathing. Dilated pupils staring through Mike at the ceiling almost shouted "Poison!"

Then Mike spotted the cause. A thin green shape slid across the floor towards the gently moving wall hangings. Mike quickly gave Keith his orders.

"Serum—in a leather case on my bed. Hurry!" He turned briefly to an Indian servant hovering ineffectually by the door. "Kill it!" he rapped in Quechua, and bent over the gasping Huascar, searching for the tiny double puncture.

For a moment Huascar seemed to be trying to focus on him, and his lips moved. Mike bent to hear what he said, but the voice was no more than a breath, and in the noise of Keith's return Mike could hardly catch the sound.

He met Keith in the doorway and took the small brown case from him, deftly extracting the hypodermic. He turned, expelling the air, and stopped dead.

Between them and Huascar stood the grey figure of the High Priest.

Mike hadn't time to argue, and tried to pass him, but Huaman blocked his way.

"None may touch the body of the Inca when the spirit has departed."

Mike would have shoved him aside, but a slight shake of Keith's head stopped him. From where he was he peered at Huascar. It was more than likely, but Mike objected on principle to taking the High Priest's word for anything! And he'd certainly arrived at the psychological moment. But Huascar lay perfectly still: the harsh breathing had stopped.

Mike stepped back. Huaman met his look boldly, then beckoned peremptorily to Keith's servant.

"Comac!"

The little Indian obeyed, and carefully lapped over the body the blanket on which Huascar lay, without actually touching him.

Comac, clearly satisfied that Huascar was dead, left the room. With a real feeling of regret, Mike replaced the syringe in its case. It was fairly obvious what had happened—an all-too-frequent tragic accident which even the twenty-four hour watch couldn't avert.

Mike went cold. Had it come so soon—and by an accident! Huascar was dead.... He looked sharply at Keith, who seemed to have had the same thought.

Two broad-shouldered guards in priestly grey tunics came with the returning Comac, but before they could take up their positions a wild-eyed, bare-footed Tupac thrust them aside. Keith's hand shot out and gripped his arm as he would have rushed past. He stopped with a jerk, and Mike felt desperately sorry for Tupac as he wrenched at Keith's iron grip. Without his feathers and most of his clothes he was hardly more than a boy—and Huascar had been his father, after all. Keith's treatment seemed a bit tough to Mike, but Keith apparently knew his man. After a moment of near frenzy Keith's calm seemed to penetrate, and with a return of his old dignity

Tupac approached the silent figure on the stone couch. Mike was even more drawn to him by this unconscious exhibition of self-discipline.

Tupac uncovered his father's face for a moment, then turned quickly and looked at the High Priest with a curious tight-lipped expression.

"How did he die?" he asked Keith.

Keith indicated the dead snake. Tupac held out his hand for it and Comac hurried to pick it up.

Tupac turned to the High Priest again, and regarded him for a moment, cold, bitter anger in his rigid face.

"Thus shall you die also, Huaman, High Priest of a serpent, slayer of kings!" And with startling vehemence he flung the dead snake at the High Priest's feet.

He turned with a look of utter loathing, and stalked to the door.

"I guess that's torn it!" Dan had arrived in the doorway, with the other two close behind.

But Huaman seemed more contemptuous than angry.

"It is for him who holds the sun in his hands to say who shall die," he said coolly.

Tupac stopped, and Mike held his breath as he recognized the subtle challenge. But Tupac didn't give the assurance Mike almost prayed for.

"Take care, High Priest: Vira-Cocha is just."

Huaman sneered openly now, and Mike's heart sank: it was too clearly the High Priest's round.

"Then let Him be just at noon!"

Mike could only guess what the High Priest meant, and when they were once more back in his room Keith cleared away any remaining doubts.

"Unless Tupac can produce the Head of Huascar by noon tomorrow I wouldn't give tuppence for his chances," he said grimly: "and the others with him."

"And it will be your fault!" G.B. was white with fury. "Why you can't leave them alone in the first place I can't think! You religious people poke yourselves in where you're not wanted—upset the settled order of generations —and those you do talk into changing their religion are let in for things like this! They'd be much happier if you left them to themselves—and what does it matter which set of rules they follow, anyway!"

Mike was nettled. "A fat lot you know about it——!"

"Take it easy, Mike!" Dan broke in. "Why not put it to one of them, G.B.?" he went on. "Comac, at least, should have an opinion."

The Indian servant came at Keith's summons, and looked at G.B. in surprise.

"Can a man think he was happy before, once he has looked into the face of the living Lord?"

"Even if it means losing a hand—or your life?" G.B. looked at him narrowly. "You would believe in Him?"

Comac smiled. "Can a man look on the sun, then say to himself, there is no sun?"

"Yes, but you haven't actually 'looked on' the Lord, as you call Him!"

The Indian touched his forehead and his heart. "But He is here. I know it. He said 'I stand at the door and knock: if any man hear My voice and open the door, I will come in to him and eat with him, and he with Me'. I opened the door—He came in."

He slipped away noiselessly into the shadows.

"That's what we bring them, G.B.," said Keith in English. "A living God, not a set of rules. A living Lord we know for ourselves. A Master Who'll expect everything you have and are—He won't take less: and Who'll help you to live to your limits—then give you the strength to push on beyond them: a God Who aims to cut out every cancerous growth of evil in your soul, and expects you to want Him to. But also a Companion Who's always standing by—closer than breathing and nearer than hands or feet—to give a steadying, helping arm. There's no one like Him, G.B. Once you've put your life in His hands He'll steer you where you'd never have dreamt of

going—but you'll go all right, because you can trust Him.
Even though you'll be called an impractical, idealistic
fool—if no worse!—sooner or later. Anybody can hit out,
with words or otherwise, but it takes somebody of His
quality to be absolute master of himself, and think of
forgiveness and mercy before petty 'own back'—and to
take an unfair laugh against himself with real good
humour. He's no God for the flabby-willed, featherbed
type: He'll toughen you up on all sides if you'll obey Him
—and it'll be by way of slog and humiliation on your part
—there are no short cuts! But all the time you'll be bound
to Him by a tie stronger than death itself—a tie that'll
make you ready to follow Him till you drop." He
shrugged. "Call it love if you like. Comac and some of the
others would cheerfully lose both hands and their feet as
well, for His sake."

There was a silence, and Mike glanced sideways at
G.B. He was twisting a piece of thread from his blanket,
and looking at the floor. After a moment he flicked the
thread away.

"All right. I can't see your point, but we'll leave it at
that. There's no sense in fighting among ourselves if we
want to get out of this in one piece."

Mike opened his mouth—and shut it again. He
wouldn't have minded getting out of it himself. It was
too obvious that Tupac didn't know where the Head of
Huascar was.

"Do you think Huascar left any record among his own
quipus?" Mike suggested hopefully. But Keith shook his
head.

"Not very likely. I've no doubt Tupac is searching at
this minute."

It occurred to Mike that Dan was unusually quiet.

"Penny for them, Dan!" he offered, more cheerfully
than he felt.

"Why do you think Tupac accused Huaman, Keith?"
said Dan. "I came on the scene a little late."

Keith shrugged. "Emotion perhaps—with a spot of wishful thinking."

"I take it that snake was the presumed cause of death, Mike?"

"Yes: no doubt about it. By the time we arrived the poison had got too much of a hold."

"Then I think Tupac was right, whether he knew it or not."

Everyone looked at Dan.

Keith's eyes narrowed. "You mean Huaman put the snake in Huascar's room?"

"I mean the snake had nothing to do with it."

That was rot—Mike knew poison symptoms when he saw them!

"I'm no expert on snakes," Dan went on, "but I've seen one or two. I wasn't sure enough before—but I am now. That one was a harmless tree snake!" He smiled. "I'm prepared to take your word that it was some kind of poison, Mike, but it wasn't snake poison. Did you find the bite?"

"No—but there wasn't time." Mike frowned. "You mean he slipped the snake in to make it look good? But why not use the genuine article? It would have looked even better—and had the same result."

"That's what has been bothering me, but I think I've got the answer. Would you have signed a death certificate for him, Mike?"

"Well, no; not unless I'd examined him personally." Mike began to see. "And Huaman wouldn't let me! But Comac and Tupac both had a close look at him, Dan."

"And do you think two Indians could tell the difference between recent death and a form of drug-induced catalepsy?"

Keith spoke across the shadowy room is Quechua. "Comac, did your master eat or drink before sleeping?"

"Only a bowl of milk."

"There's your method," said Dan. "Simple enough to

tamper with it—they're not reared on crime stories here."

"Why bother to drug him when he could have got rid of him outright?" said Mike.

Keith smiled slightly. "He's only got to keep him out of the way for another day, and he's got the people, but—and remember to Huaman there's a strong sneaking 'but'—if the spirit of Huascar should turn nasty, he can produce the Inca unharmed. If the spirit of Huascar doesn't, then he can quietly dispose of him and no one will know any difference."

"Does Gregory come into all this somewhere?" said Mike. "If he has had any hand in it, it looks as though he's tripped himself up. He's lost all chance of finding the very thing he's after if the secret dies with Huascar."

"That's one good reason why I doubt if Huascar is dead," said Dan. "It seems a pretty good bargain to me. Huaman gets the city, by Gregory's strategy, and Gregory gets the 'light' to take away where it can't do Huaman any harm in the future—always assuming, of course, that he can get it out of Huascar."

"He hasn't got it yet," said Mike hopefully. "Tupac might find it first." He was beginning to feel he'd had enough for one day—and there was an irritatingly elusive thought at the back of his mind which wouldn't settle long enough for him to grasp it. A thought he ought to grasp.

"We can't do anything now in any case," said Keith. "Huascar is safe so long as he is on view in the temple—which he will be for two days." He stood up. "John Akobe and I are going to have a word with Tupac. I suggest you turn in for a few hours."

Mike wasn't sorry—even his stone couch seemed inviting. He and Dan walked along the corridor with G.B.

"You still think we ought to leave it alone, G.B.?" said Dan.

"I'm sorry—yes. So long as Gregory doesn't get the 'light' I honestly don't care what happens. It's hard luck if any of the Indians have to suffer for it—but you know my views on that." His mouth snapped, and that was that.

Mike stood for a long time by his window, looking down over the bunched roofs on the terraces below. That elusive thought bothered him: but at last he gave it up and went to bed, more tired than he realized.

Suddenly—it must have been only a short time later—he woke with a start, his heart racing. His lamp had burned out, and the only light in the room came from the thick stars.

He lay perfectly still, controlling his tingling nerves by sheer force of will. It was quiet now, but something had woken him—something close at hand in his room.

With every sense abnormally alert he strained his eyes and ears in the dimness.

A faint, vaguely familiar smell wafted to him.

7

MIKE REMEMBERS

MIKE's brain worked overtime on that smell—a sweet, smoky smell. Herbs! That was it! The herbs in the temple! He shot up on the couch—and immediately his arms were seized from behind in a grip which held him helpless. A hand slipped over his mouth and something cold and hard touched his throat. A soft chuckle of triumph came from the darkness behind him, and a voice spoke quickly and quietly in English.

"Don't call out, Mr. Brent: you'd be dead before anyone arrived."

Mike's wrists were tied tightly behind, and the hand and knife were withdrawn.

"I'll take your word for that—Gregory!" Mike was disgusted that he had been taken so easily. He couldn't see the High Priest, but he knew he was there somewhere by that scent in his robe.

Gregory came from behind and sat on the edge of the couch. Mike eyed him with considerable interest despite the sticky situation. He was much younger than Mike had expected, having in mind the crippled Museum attendant: hardly older than Dan. But he was curiously ordinary to look at. The first requisite in spies, Mike thought, the ability to go unnoticed. Gregory would certainly do that: it was too dark to see his colouring at all, but he looked wholly unremarkable. But, as Mike knew too well, it was all more than balanced by a completely extraordinary brain.

"I suggest you don't pull too much with your wrists," Gregory said pleasantly. "It won't add to your comfort. Now then, Brent," he went on crisply: "I want the Head of Huascar, and I'm quite ready to do more or less anything to get it." Mike had no doubts about that. "The High Priest is quite agreeable to my taking it well away—and is even prepared to help me get it, in exchange for—for my help in his own affairs."

Mike snorted.

"Now then," said Gregory again: "I understand that Huascar won't wake up for four days—that idiot of a High Priest overdid it!" he added irritably. "Which is unfortunate, because I can't wait that long. Which means also that now only one person knows where the Head of Huascar is." He leaned forward suddenly and tapped Mike's chest. "And that one is you, Mr. Brent."

"Me!" Mike was speechless.

Gregory's hand flashed out and gripped Mike by the throat, forcing his head back on the blankets.

"Don't play with me!" The easy manner changed to a savage snarl. "I've no time for it!"

He snapped out an order in the dialect, and Huaman came for the first time into Mike's view, to hand Gregory a slim-necked jar.

"Watch this, Brent!"

Gregory tipped the flask so that a drop of liquid fell on to Mike's cover. With a faint hiss the threads shrivelled, leaving a small hole, smoking slightly.

"The effect would be the same on anything, of course."

Despite the almost airless warmth in the small room Mike's forehead went cold. There was no doubt at all as to what was in Gregory's mind.

"You have just ten seconds to tell me where the Head is," said Gregory. "That should be long enough."

"Don't be a blithering idiot, Gregory!" Mike was genuinely bewildered. "I haven't got anything to tell you——!"

"Then you had better think of something, hadn't you!" Gregory's eyes were cold and very hard, and not so ordinary as Mike had thought. "I want that Head, Brent!"

Mike began to see red—it was all such rubbish!

"Then you'd better ask someone who knows where it is! Huascar didn't confide his State secrets to me!"

Gregory looked at him curiously. "Didn't he?" The question was silky smooth.

"You're off your nut!" Mike turned his head away in exasperation. "Even Incas who think they're dying don't choose me to tell their secrets to! I'm not—" He stopped suddenly.

Gregory smiled. "I see you have remembered something."

Mike had remembered all right! That elusive thought was suddenly crystal clear—a few breathed words—so weak they were hardly words at all. . . .

Mike shut his teeth.

"Ten seconds," said Gregory softly.

"Go ride your bike."

There was a faint trickling sound from below Mike's field of vision, and some drops of moisture oozed from Mike's forehead. This was getting nasty.

Huaman handed Gregory a seal of twisted metal, like a flat snake.

"Apparently this is Xicchu's trade mark, for use on people of whom he doesn't approve." Gregory smiled at Mike. "I hardly think he would approve of you." He dipped it in the bowl of liquid on the floor, and let it drip off. "Now then." His tone was cool and businesslike. "You know what I want, Brent—the rest is up to you."

Mike shut his teeth again and sent up a silent SOS.

A brief order, and Huaman gripped Mike's chin in hard hands, pinning his head back.

"Just a sample," said Gregory kindly—and something bit savagely into Mike's chest.

His involuntary cry was strangled by the grip on his chin, but as his body jerked his foot caught the heavy jar at the foot of the couch. It toppled and broke with a crash against the stone wall.

The seal was withdrawn abruptly. "Not a sound!" Gregory hissed his warning in the dialect, and again the blade was pressed against Mike's throat. For an endless moment only a quick breathing broke the silence, then there were footsteps outside. Gregory bent swiftly and picked up the bowl of liquid.

The door curtains parted and G.B.'s pained face looked in.

"What do you think you're—"

His jaw dropped as he caught sight of Gregory. "What—!"

"Keep still!" Gregory's low tone discouraged any argument. He stood over Mike with the bowl in his hands. "Brent, tell your friend that if he calls out, attacks me, or brings anyone else I shall tip this over."

G.B. moved as though to come in.

"No—!" Mike almost choked. "Do as he says, G.B.!" G.B. hesitated for a moment, then ducked back through the curtains.

There was a movement near the window, and Gregory turned sharply. Mike's heart pounded as a slop of the liquid hit the bed, barely missing him. He heard a low-voiced argument, then Huaman slipped noiselessly away. Gregory turned back to Mike.

"Our friend is afraid—for his good name," he sneered. He held the bowl up and looked at it.

"Mr. Brooke's interruption has given me an idea."

Mike stared doggedly at the ceiling. This was even nastier—and if the truth were known, he hadn't the nerve to look at that bowl, only an arm's length from him.

A rivulet of moisture trickled down his face.

"This is your last chance, Brent. Either you tell me where the Head is, or I tip this up—slowly."

Mike's teeth were shut so tightly they hurt. He knew two minutes are enough if God is in them—but they can seem a mighty long time!

Then his heart almost stopped. From the corner of his eye he caught a movement of the door curtain. It took all his will power to give no sign. He swallowed.

"Aren't—aren't you going to give me ten seconds this time?"

Gregory looked at him in surprise. He shrugged. "If you want them. What are ten seconds?"

A short black tube was slowly coming through the curtains. He had to gain time!

"But—but you—I can't die like this!" His voice was almost a croak. "I—I haven't got my boots on!"

Gregory scowled. "What are you talking about?"

"I've always said I wanted to die with my boots on."

Gregory smiled. "Then I'm sorry I can't oblige you. Now then—that's enough fooling! One——"

"Wait a minute! If I die you may never know!"

Gregory smiled again. "You probably won't—quite. Two——"

The explosion splintered the darkness, and Gregory stared foolishly at the pieces of shattered bowl in his hands.

G.B. rushed in, but Gregory got in first with a blow which sent G.B. reeling. Gregory made for the window and slipped nimbly through.

"I haven't finished with you yet, Brent!"

G.B. picked himself up.

"Darkest hour before the dawn—can't see a thing!" he muttered. "Ah, that's better." His oilskinned match flared for a moment. "What—!" He stared at the smouldering hole in the edge of Mike's blankets. "Is that what he was threatening to tip on you! Mike, what's been happening?"

"The filthy hound!" was G.B.'s simple reaction to Mike's explanation.

Dan appeared in the doorway. "Are you all right, Mike? I thought I heard a shot!"

92

"You did," said Mike wryly, rubbing his stiff wrists.

The others' reactions were similar to G.B.'s when Mike had told his story again. "What did Huascar say?" said Dan. "We'll have to let Tupac know at once!"

"Ho no!" said Mike. "After this, the fewer who know, the better! I'll tell him myself."

Dan nodded grimly without argument. "Right. Come on then: we won't let you—or Tupac—out of our sight until he is actually standing out there with the 'light' in his hands!"

G.B. frowned at them.

"You're going to take the risk then, still, of Gregory getting hold of it?" He punched his forehead suddenly with an air of desperation. "Can't you get it into your thick heads that the trouble as it is will go no further than this dot on the map! If Gregory gets the 'light' there'll be no end! You're just doing his job for him!"

Dan's eyes narrowed at G.B. for a second.

"Right!" he said tersely. "It comes down to this: we've got to decide—and quickly!—just how much we can really stake in hard facts on our belief in the reality of our God. If we believe that He can and will take charge of operations—then we'll push on. If we're not prepared to trust Him with those hard facts, then we can only take G.B.'s advice, which from that point of view is the only possible course." He looked at them each in turn. "Keith? John Akobe?" There was no hesitation. "And Mike?"

But that was easier said than done. They would be launching out, trusting to something they couldn't see, couldn't feel—couldn't even prove existed!—against a proven vicious strength.

He was conscious that his God was waiting for his decision, as well as the others.

He drew a deep breath, and winced at the touch of his shirt. "Right-ho, Dan: you can count me in."

"I'm sorry, G.B. The Ayes have it. But you needn't feel obliged to have any part in it."

G.B. shrugged. "I think you're all walking a very shaky tightrope. You'll need all the help you can get—so you'd better count me in as well—but not for the same hare-brained reason!"

"As you say." Dan turned to Mike. "Are you up to it now, Mike?"

Tupac listened intently to Mike's story.

"Beneath the sacred pool: you are sure those are my father's words, my white brother?"

"Quite sure. Do you know where that is?"

Tupac nodded. "The sacred pool lies in the house of shadows beneath the temple." He smiled suddenly. "I, too, share your trust in the Great Spirit. I go to find the Head of Huascar."

And despite G.B.'s cynical eyebrows Mike was prepared to trust Tupac's motives.

"We'll come with you and keep an eye open," said Keith.

"I don't like that rumbling," Dan muttered as they followed Tupac through austere empty rooms, where the sound echoed hollowly from the stone walls.

"Nor do I," said Keith. "It's worse than I've known it since I've been here. More frequent."

Tupac halted at last, and pulled aside a rug. Mike looked into the exposed gaping hole, and resolved privately to keep well behind Tupac in future. Sudden drops were too popular in these parts!

They followed Tupac down a short flight of stone steps into a narrow passage. It was almost as dark as the temple, and lit in the same way, by lamps which flickered in the draught of their passing. Mike shivered. It was damp, too. He felt the wall. They were underground all right, but the passage was smooth, and clearly man-made.

The rumbling was louder down here. If they were going towards the temple it would probably get louder still. Mike knew you could get surprisingly close to a volcano without any damage—so long as it did no more than rumble!—but it was a pretty uncomfortable feeling just the same to know that the earth was boiling not so very far beneath your feet!

The passages began to grow complicated, and soon Mike lost all sense of direction. It was really damp now, and here and there water trickled down the walls.

"I should think we're about under the temple," said Keith in reply to Mike's query.

More steps led down into a large chamber, which Mike noticed was partly natural cave, and Tupac stopped.

"There is the sacred pool," he said.

Mike wasn't very impressed—at least, not by the pool, large as it was. But the setting gave it the needed supernatural flavour; and again he could appreciate the reason for its sacredness to the Indians. The vast echoing bare rock, the flickering lamps and black shadows, the continuous slow drip-drip-drip from somewhere in the dimness, and, above all, the silence of the black water, had their effect even on him.

"'Beneath the sacred pool'," Tupac repeated softly as they stood looking down into it.

"Is it deep?" said Keith, and Tupac shook his head.

"I don't know."

Tupac didn't seem very keen to go any nearer, so Mike rolled up his shirt sleeve, and felt down gingerly into the water. His arm disappeared to the shoulder before he drew it out.

"Ugh—it's cold! But it looks like a swim for somebody."

"That's not likely," said Keith; "mountain Indians can't usually swim. It must be somewhere that can be reached from the edge. We'll feel round the sides—there may be a ledge or something."

Mike kept an eye on G.B. as they lay feeling under the black water, but it was Keith who found it. Mike felt a thrill of expectancy as Keith drew it out—and he wasn't disappointed.

An exquisite life-sized skull of rock crystal lay in Keith's dripping hands, and in its translucent brain cavity the 'light' was already beginning to glow by the faint lamps. Mike was a little put off his stroke by the beauty of the thing.

Keith handed it to Tupac, who also seemed overawed, though more probably by its significance than its appearance. For a moment they stood in silence, looking at the Head of Huascar.

"Thank you, Mr. Oban," said a smooth voice from somewhere near the steps.

Mike didn't need to look round: Gregory's voice was almost recorded in his eardrums. He gave Tupac a shove backwards, and planted himself in front of him.

But there were too many grey tunics closing in on them.

Gregory stood with thumbs hooked in his belt, smiling his satisfaction.

Keith joined Mike to make a barrier in front of Tupac, and all three backed watchfully away beyond the pool.

"I want that skull, Tupac."

Mike flexed his fists. "Come and get it!" But he knew they were well outnumbered. G.B. and his revolver were already out of action. Their only chance was in surprise. Almost before the idea had formed, he snatched the skull from Tupac. With it tucked under his left arm like a rugger ball he put his head down and charged the approaching 'priests' like a line of backs. The first reeled back from a vigorous hand-off, the second doubled up with a fist in his stomach. There was only one way out that Mike knew— and he made for it.

He tore up the steps and into the passage. His footsteps echoed loudly between the narrow walls. He glanced back —the priests were surging up after him. A passage led off to the right, and Mike tore down it. If he met somebody it would be just too bad! Another passage turned left. If only he wasn't wearing boots! He stopped for a second to listen. He had left them some way behind, but they were still on his track. His lips tightened grimly. They were as much priests as he was—you didn't get a physique like that from just attending Services! And they were too disciplined! There was no shouting—only the businesslike beat of sandals on the stone floor. He set off again as quietly as he could. The passage seemed to lead nowhere, except to other passages running off in all directions. All were lit by the same dim lamps—and all looked alike.

They were still after him! He had to get rid of those boots! He stopped where he was and desperately tugged them off. He'd have to leave them—no, they'd show which way he'd gone! He ran on, stuffing the skull in the top of one, and tucking them under his arm. The shock of the cold floor freshened him, and he hurried on round the next two corners. He stopped to listen again, gulping air. They were further away! He missed the next two openings and ran down a third.

Mike realized the square stone passages had given way to irregular living rock, roughly smoothed. He must be going away from the city into the mountain. He turned round, but the first passage he took was a dead end. He wandered in a maze, sometimes touching the hewn and sometimes the living rock. The passages were too well kept. There was no dust to show him which way he had come—though, on second thoughts, it wouldn't show his pursuers either. There had been no sound of them for some time now.

The familiar mark of a serpent over the entrance to one of the natural passages gave him an idea. He looked at the skull.

"The sooner I get rid of you the better, old mate. This looks a reasonable spot—Tupac probably knows how to find it again as it's marked."

He placed the skull in a niche a few metres inside the passage, blowing out the nearest lamps to keep the 'light' from giving itself away; and put on his boots again.

At last, after at least another hour or more's wandering, completely lost, he emerged hot and dishevelled—into the open air!

Mike stared round him, startled. He was on one of the lower levels of the city, just inside the wall. He couldn't stay out there! The sun would be up soon and he'd have no cover. He flattened himself against the wall in the deepest shadow, and thought desperately. He was on his own now. The people might not be hostile—yet—but he wasn't going to risk it! And Gregory wasn't likely to let him slip so easily. Comac! He'd have to find Comac. The little Indian, at least, would be on their side!

He slid along by the wall. It was apparently too early for many people to be about, and he managed to dodge those he did see, mostly on their way down to the terraces with their 'hoes' over broad bronzed shoulders.

He wandered for twenty minutes trying to work his way back to the palace without being seen. Not meeting any-one on the higher levels he became over-confident, and turned a corner without first reconnoitring by ear.

He came face to face with a party of priests.

8

THE TRAITOR

THEN it began all over again. After the first shock of surprise the priests belted down the stairway after Mike. There seemed to be a delay of some kind at one corner, and he gained twenty metres. He toiled frantically up the next stairway. Suddenly a face appeared round a house. Mike pulled up sharply, but a handless arm beckoned him on. It was Comac.

Mike glanced behind. One of the younger priests was standing at the turn in the stairway—watching him. Mike's heart sank. But even as he looked back the priest turned round and beckoned the others on—across the end of the stairway! Mike dived after Comac, his heart nearly choking him.

The little Indian held up his good hand, and they flattened against the wall listening to the dwindling sounds of pursuit.

"But he must have seen me!" Mike gasped when they relaxed a little at last.

"Yes, he saw. But he is one of us."

"A Christian? Among the priests!"

"He has not yet found courage to speak of his belief."

"I can understand that!" said Mike grimly. "I guess it would mean instant—" he made an expressive gesture—"if he did."

"Not instant," said Comac, and left it at that.

"Where are we going?" said Mike, as they emerged cautiously into the street. "And how did you happen to be standing by so conveniently?"

"I have been looking for you. I'll take you to the secret chambers beneath the palace. You'll be safe there. The other white men and the black are prisoners, but alive. They——"

The wailing of a horn broke in on Comac's words.

"The temple horn!" He stared at Mike in amazed alarm. "Xicchu's summons to all the people. It has not been heard for many years!"

The compelling note was repeated three times. Comac changed direction, and in a few minutes Mike found himself on a high terrace overlooking the square, but hidden from below by bushes. The square was filling quickly with men, from the houses, and hurrying up from the terraces again. They gathered in front of the temple, and their expectant buzzing reached Mike as a faint hum.

Soon the High Priest appeared through the doorway, followed by his grey bodyguard. Mike felt "appeared" was the only word for his entrance. He stood motionless on the top step for a calculated moment as anticipation rippled into silence over the now considerable crowd.

Mike suddenly sensed real, bad trouble, and every nerve quivered into alertness.

Huaman raised his arms, in another calculated gesture.

"People of Xicchu—I, the High Priest of Xicchu, bring you good tidings!" His voice trembled with a nicely subdued intensity. "Huascar is dead—rejected by the spirit of Huascar—slain by the mighty hand of Xicchu!" The people murmured excitedly—and Mike suddenly saw the reason for the snake in Huascar's room. Snakes would be Xicchu's agents! Huaman went on, his intensity less subdued this time.

"Now also is the son of Huascar!"

There was a ragged shout from the crowd.

Mike could see it happening before his eyes: a powerful personality skilfully playing on the emotions of a simple people who didn't realize what was happening to them.

Huaman flung up his arms fiercely to the rising sun. "Xicchu has slain the unbelievers!"

Mike went cold. The High Priest's object was clear now. A shout of "Xicchu!" had broken from the crowd:

Huaman raised his arms again, passionately taking up their shout——

"Xicchu is Lord!"

The crowd roared, waving fists adding force to their acclaim.

Then the unexpected happened. There was a sudden movement among the 'bodyguard', and one of them rushed down in front of the Hight Priest. Even from that distance Mike recognized him, and held his breath. The young priest held out his arms to the people.

"No, people of Xicchu!" he cried; "Xicchu is not Lord! The High Priest speaks falsely. Xicchu did not kill Huascar—" The crowd growled ominously "—Xicchu is nothing!" His voice choked off as Huaman jerked him backwards. The man struggled, trying to call out. "Not Xicchu—" he gasped "—Vira-Cocha—!" But his words were cut off in a rush of priests.

Mike felt sick: he was completely helpless to do anything to stop this. He could see it coming, as inevitable as night and day. It always did. Soon they'd be an uncontrollable mob, howling for something—anything—to destroy.

Huaman waved his arms over his head: he seemed infected with his own fever.

"Destroy the unbelievers! Seize them! Let not one remain to pollute the city of the great Xicchu! Xicchu shall slay the blasphemers! Seize them!"

To Mike's horror self-control snapped at once. The cry ran like a flame through the dense crowd. It was like watching a ghastly play, high up and detached from the characters. But this was no play. Men were being cleverly whipped into an hysteria which could only end one way. And Mike was completely powerless to do anything about it.

Oh no, the High Priest wasn't carried away—his move-

ments were too effective for that! He was turning these
people back into savages, and knew exactly what he was
doing. Urged on by his now wild gesticulating the burly
priests ran down the steps. The cry "Xicchu!—Destroy
the unbelievers!" rose in waves all over the square, gathering force with each burst. The crowd became a heaving,
shouting mass, inflamed by Huaman's increasingly fren-
zied shrieking.

Mike was stiff with apprehension. He had noticed a
small group standing a little apart towards the right of the
temple steps. The crowd hadn't seen them yet.

All at once he became conscious that Comac was looking at him with a bewildered expression, which Mike
didn't understand.

"Will you not save them?" Comac said.

"Me?"

"You are a white man—a servant of Vira-Cocha—the
Lord Jesus."

Mike stared at the scene below. The crowd surged back
and forth across the now half sunlit square, its movements
not yet co-ordinated.

"What could I do against that—it would be suicide to
go down there!"

"You are a white man," Comac repeated simply; "one
who walks with Vira-Cocha."

Mike thought furiously. Dan had once remarked that
however tight the situation God could always show His
children a way through.

The scene below was changing now. The crowd had
suddenly spotted the little knot by the steps. Trapped between the temple and the mob they stared round desperately; then apparently seeing no possible way of escape
they turned back, and stood quite still, close together,
waiting calmly. The front rank of the rush slowed in the
face of their calm, and Huaman half lifted his arms again.

Suddenly, with a rumble like an avalanche, the growling mountain spoke. The crowd froze, silenced, as thunder

rolled from the heart of the rock and shook the ground.

Mike squinted into the clear sky. A thousand metres up a small plume of smoke detached itself from the peak, and drifted away like a grey ghost.

As the rumble died away Huaman flung his arms wide.

"Enough, enough, O people of Xicchu! Ye hear the voice of the great god! He is satisfied this dawn with his people's service!"

"That's quick thinking," Mike muttered. "He could see his massacre misfiring on him!"

"But at noon—!" The crowd shouted in anticipation, regaining their enthusiasm—and Mike caught the glint of sunlight on a waving blade. "Seek them out—drive them from their holes! Xicchu shall be doubly satisfied at noon!"

Forced to be satisfied that its victims were secure in the priests' hands, the crowd turned and trampled its way across the square towards the houses of the city.

Mike stared after them. That glint of sunlight was the first sign. The mob's resentment at being cheated would soon come to the top; it wouldn't be satisfied with mere prisoners much longer. They'd left Huaman behind now; and now he needn't even pretend to restrain them. He'd set the reaction going: now it would work itself out in the inevitable way. And he could wash his hands of the whole thing! It was a move worthy of Gregory.

An idea began to form in Mike's mind. "If only we could get all the Christians in one place somehow!" he muttered.

Comac took him up eagerly. "Those who did not obey the temple summons will be gathered before Vira-Cocha. I will show you the way!"

Mike felt a twinge. This little Indian who had already sampled their savagery was ready to go down and risk it all over again, while he was concentrating on his own skin. He looked down at the empty square. Huaman was turning back into the temple, his smile just discernible.

"I'll show you the way!" Comac repeated.

Mike shook his head irritably. "It's impossible! What could we do against that mob! We'd only get ourselves caught as well—and what good would that do anybody?" He forced himself to meet Comac's disappointed look.

"But our brother Keith tells us it is written in the sacred Book that nothing shall be impossible with the Lord. Does the sacred Book not speak true words then, white man who knows the ways of Vira-Cocha?"

Mike's mouth tightened. "Yes—it speaks true words."

"Then why do you not believe it? If the white men do not believe, how can the men of Xicchu do so?"

Mike looked down again at the square, and took a deep breath.

"All right," he said; "we'll go."

He felt no intrepid hero as he followed the little Indian down the deserted upper terraces. As they hurried around intricate narrow stairways they could hear shouts above them on the other side of the little city.

Comac stopped at last at a low thatched house in the obviously poorer quarter on the lowest terrace. They listened. The shouts were too near for comfort now.

"Hurry, Comac: we haven't much time! We've got to get them out before the mob arrives. We'll hide them beneath the palace until we can find a way out."

Mike followed Comac into the stuffy house. Excited voices came from behind a curtained doorway. Comac pushed it aside, and a dead, horrified silence fell. A small group of frightened brown faces stared at them. Mike unconsciously estimated the number—fifteen, eleven men, four women. A sixteenth who had apparently been addressing them leaned against the wall, clutching a badly gashed arm. Mike shuddered. He had been right: they weren't stopping at capture now.

An elderly Indian came forward.

"My brother," he said gravely, his lined, weatherbeaten face almost triumphant now that the blow had apparently fallen: "we do not fear what you may do to our bodies, for our souls you cannot touch."

Mike suddenly came to. "Comac—they think—tell them, quickly, who I am!"

Comac spoke too urgently for Mike to catch all he said. But he saw the bewildered, unbelieving looks darted from one to the other of them.

His scalp prickled. "Comac!—tell them there's no time to lose! Once those blighters catch sight of us we'll all be as good as—as—" The Quechua for 'cold mutton' escaped him.

The old man regarded them quietly. "Comac, yes, we know: but this white man. How do we know he serves Vira-Cocha? One of the white men is evil." A shout reached them from the streets. "Perhaps he is come to lead us to those who would destroy us."

"There'll be no need in a minute!" Mike groaned inwardly. "Convince them, Lord——!"

Suddenly Comac leapt at him, and before he could move his shirt was ripped open.

"There my brothers—see the mark of Xicchu—only put on those he would punish!"

The group of Christians gathered round to see.

The old man was contrite. "What would you have us do, our brother?" he said humbly.

Mike tore a strip from his already tattered shirt. "Tell them what we plan to do, and tell them to *hurry!*" He left the talking to Comac while he bound the wounded Indian's arm as swiftly as he could: though he could tell there was little he could do for him without a transfusion unit.

The shouting was dangerously near as they slipped out of the house, Comac and the elder leading, and Mike bringing up the rear.

They hurried up the empty stairways, the weakened Indian stumbling and holding on to Mike. Once they fell so far behind that the others stopped to wait for them. In those few moments the noise of pursuit doubled.

The wounded man was about all in.

"I—hold you back," he panted. "They will catch us." He shook free from Mike. "Go on—I'll come as I can."

There were cries of protest, and one or two of nervous irritation, but the young Indian leaned on the wall and refused to budge. Mike tried to haul him along, but he hooked his good arm into a window opening. There was no time to argue—the mob was too close—and there were fifteen other lives at stake. Mike decided quickly with tight lips. He put all he could into a quick, gruff grip, and hurried the others on.

They glanced back as they turned the next bend, but the young man had gone. The shouts of the mob suddenly grew more excited, and exultant cries conveyed clearly what had happened: he had given them a few minutes' advantage.

Mike's last prejudice against the humanity of these brown people withered: colour was ultimately meaningless, and even to consider it was sometimes near-blasphemy.

"How much further, Comac?"

"Two stairs, then we are at the palace."

Comac led them cautiously through empty palace rooms. The breakdown was complete: even Huascar's servants had gone with the mob, except any who were among the first few to be taken. Mike recognized the way Tupac had taken them before, but they turned off earlier, passed down another flight of steps—and once more Mike found himself in the comparative safety of the damp underground chambers.

Comac still led the way through the warren of passages, and came to a halt in a small bare stone room.

"We may rest here." Comac set the example by dropping flat on his back. Mike sat on the floor with his back to the cold wall and wiped the sweat out of his eyes, unobtrusively taking professional note of the company. They were all exhausted, but in reasonable shape otherwise.

Well, the race was on now, all right. The High Priest

had jumped the gun for some reason—Gregory had probably given him the confidence. It suddenly occurred to Mike that the Lord had got them out of it after all—the first stage, anyway. But it wasn't over yet! They couldn't stay down there for ever . . . !

Mike slid across to Comac, and spoke softly.

"Can you take care of them, Comac? We'll have to think of what to do later, when they've rested a bit. I'm going to try and find out what has happened to Keith and the others." Comac nodded. "I'll make a mark on the wall as I go to guide me back."

Mike set off in what Comac told him was the direction of the temple, scratching X-es on the wall with a chip of stone.

"Mike!"

He stood stock still. It was very faint but unmistakable.

"Mike—where are you?" The call echoed weirdly along the passages.

G.B.! Mike listened. It was a few minutes before the cry was repeated, wearily, as though G.B. had been calling for a long time.

"Mike!"

Yes, it was G.B. all right, but a good way off!

"G.B.!" Mike shouted at the top of his voice.

"Mike—where are you?" G.B. had heard him.

"I don't know—keep shouting!"

A few yards at a time the voice grew louder, and at last rounding a corner——

"G.B.!"

"Mike!"

"G.B.—what's happened! Are you all right? And the others?"

"Yes—yes, we're all right." G.B.'s enthusiasm seemed to evaporate suddenly, and he hardly met Mike's eye. "Yes, we're all right," he repeated. "Where have you been, Mike?"

Mike told him briefly of his doings over the past few hours. "And they're hidden away snugly at the end of the line of X-es!" he finished triumphantly.

G.B. looked at the scratches with a peculiar expression.

"G.B.—are you sure you're all right?"

G.B. stared at the marks.

"Yes, quite all right. Is—is that your route-marking, as it were?"

"That's it. Come on: I'll show you if you like. You could do with a rest by the look of you." G.B.'s arm stiffened in his grasp. "What's up?—don't you want to come?"

"Yes—I'll come."

There was certainly something very wrong with G.B. but it didn't seem the right moment for probing, so Mike led the way in silence.

Comac remembered G.B. and reassured the others.

"And these are all the Christians left—in the city?" G.B. faltered as Comac ended his version of their story.

"So far as we know, yes," said Mike. G.B.'s queerly apathetic attitude worried him.

G.B. stared at the floor, the corners of his mouth twitching down for a moment.

"I'm sorry, Mike," he murmured, and went back to the doorway; and in a flash Mike understood. He sprang after him, but it was too late.

The grey priests poured in, hopelessly outnumbering them.

"Thank you, Mr. Brooke," said Gregory at last, smiling at G.B. "You've done very well—I couldn't have managed better myself. Certainly not more thoroughly."

9

ULTIMATUM

MIKE was stupefied. Stumbling along the passage between four muscular priests, he tried to think straight, but
his brain wouldn't focus. G.B. had deliberately handed
them over. No, it wasn't possible. But he had let Mike lead
him to the others—even made sure they were all there!—
then calmly turned round and——

Mike suddenly saw red.

"Why you—you—Judas!" he gritted. The grip on his
arms held him back. "You'll pay for this!" A dull flush at
the back of G.B.'s neck showed he had heard, but he didn't
answer.

Gregory looked back, smiling his smoothest.

"Come, come, Brent: forgive them that trespass against
you. Your Christian duty, you know!"

Mike clenched his fists. "I'll give you Christian duty if I
get my hands on you—!"

Gregory laughed. "I think you would, too!"

Mike glanced behind at the exhausted group dragging
wearily along. Only Comac seemed hopeful, and he
smiled wanly at Mike.

"The tale is not yet told, my brother. The Great Spirit
is good. If the good white men trust Him, then who are we
to disbelieve?" His simplicity made Mike feel ashamed.

There was a faint murmur of assent from the others, and
they brightened for a moment. Mike caught a brief, almost triumphant, expression on Gregory's face, but
couldn't work out the reason for it, just then.

Mike felt sick with helplessness again. Not so much for

himself as for these people. He had led them into a trap, yet they still looked to him to lead them. No situation so tight the Lord couldn't think of a way through ... it was hard to believe from where he was.

The passage ended in a low crypt-like chamber.

"Mike!"

They were all there.

At a sign from Gregory, who seemed to have taken over, the Indians were hauled to the wall and fastened with a primitive version of handcuffs. Mike found himself standing next to Dan, his back to the wall and his wrists locked on either side of his head.

"You can cool off here for a while," was Gregory's parting shot. "Come along, Mr. Brooke."

No one spoke until they were alone again.

"Thank God you're all right, Mike!" said Dan. "What happened to you?"

Mike told his story for the second time.

"I'll wring his neck for him!" he finished savagely.

Keith smiled briefly. "Don't judge him too hardly, Mike: some men's breaking point comes earlier than others'."

"He should have put up with anything first!"

Keith shrugged. "Gregory is fairly inventive. Anyhow, there's no point in discussing what ought to have happened. Thing is, what do we do now?"

"You've tried breaking these handcuff things, I suppose?" Mike wrenched at the immovable metal embedded in the stone.

"John Akobe did, but they caught him and chained him as well." Dan looked thoughtful. "Mike, you say Huaman stopped the mob when the mountain rumbled?"

Mike snorted. "He could see the effect was pegging out on him, that's why! The Christians weren't afraid when it came to it. He grabbed at the chance to save his face! But he didn't really stop them." He listened. "It's certainly loud down here."

"But he had those—at least—taken alive?" Dan went on. "What do you think, Keith?"

Keith shrugged again. "At best they'll be the noon sacrifice, and us with them. If they're all like Comac and that priest there's not much else for Huaman to do."

"That's reckoning without Gregory."

"Exactly. I said 'at best'. Mike, you still know where the skull is, don't you?"

Mike remembered the skull with a shock. "I'm the only one who does now—again! My hat, we've got to get out of this!"

He pulled at the metal bands, but they were too strong.

"I knew a trick once," he muttered; "they do it in India. How to compress your fingers. If I could still do it— half a minute—you stretch your thumb first—you try it— then all your fingers close together round it and—it's coming—I think!" For an agonizing moment his thumb joint wedged, then, with a crack—"Done it!"

"No good—I can't do it," said Dan ruefully.

"'The bones of the old elephant are not so supple as those of the young gazelle'," John Akobe observed gravely.

Dan grinned. "Not so much of the old elephant, John Akobe! It's no good, Mike, you can't do anything with ours without the key-thing. Hop it while the going's good —and, Mike, go easy with G.B. if you find him: at least until you know what's behind it."

Mike snorted, though he knew Dan was right, really, and made for the flight of steps up which the others had gone. He might be able to get hold of the keys—or whatever they used—somehow. He cautiously pushed up a corner of the rug covering the opening over his head.

The small room at the top of the steps was empty, but he could hear voices through the curtained doorway opposite. Sliding along by the wall he moved the curtain back a fraction of an inch.

It was apparently Huaman's private room. Huaman himself sat on a rug sideways to the window, his eyes fixed on Gregory, who perched in the opening. Mike's blood boiled at the sight of him. A movement to the left caught his eye. G.B., seemingly unrestricted, sat on some blankets on the floor, with forearms on knees, staring at nothing.

"You're a fool," said Gregory calmly. He spoke in easy dialect. Huaman's face darkened, but he made no move. "I suppose you think when you've put them to death your troubles will be over!" Without giving the Hight Priest a chance to reply he went on softly, almost thinking aloud. "Oh no! There will be one—a boy—or an old man—who has been overlooked as harmless, and before you know it the place will be crawling with them again!" His mouth curled into a snarl. "I know them—you don't. Killing them is no good; Christians thrive on it! They always have."

"They will not thrive at noon: Xicchu's fangs are sharp."

Gregory waved the interruption aside irritably. "Xicchu! You don't believe in Xicchu any more than I do!"

"Perhaps not, but he serves my purpose. And so long as the people believe in him—" Huaman shrugged expressively.

Gregory turned on him.

"Exactly—so long as the people believe! And unless you destroy these—these Christians it won't be long before Xicchu is as dead as the Great Inca!"

"Destroy, but not kill?" Huaman was sarcastic, but Gregory chose to ignore it.

"There is only one way to destroy them—from inside. Divide them, discourage them, show them their own weakness, or better still the weakness of those they expect to be strong." Gregory smiled slowly, with the same triumphant look Mike had caught in the passage. "Yes, those they expect to be strong. You Indians can't move a step without a white man behind you. Begin with the white men!"

G.B. looked up suddenly, but his eyes dropped when they met Gregory's.

Huaman regarded Gregory curiously. "I do not delude myself the white man cares for the affairs of Xicchu—yet his brow is moist as he plans to destroy the followers of the God called Jesus. Why should this be?"

Gregory's lip curled again. "So long as they believe their God is with them nothing can touch them! You can tear them to pieces and they'll only thank you for it. You saw them today when the first shock of your fool massacre had passed." His voice sank to harshness. "I want to show them there are places where their God can't help them—that they are as destructible as anybody else!"

"And perhaps the white man wishes to prove this to himself also," said Huaman silkily. He shrugged contemptuously. "I don't fear them or their God, but the plan is good."

Mike stiffened as Huaman rose, but they went through another door to the left. Gregory turned back to G.B., who stood disconsolately in the middle of the room.

"You know you are quite free to go where you like, Brooke—so long as you don't try to undo any of your good work."

Mike made sure the coast was clear, then stepped into the room. G.B. spun round, startled.

"Well, G.B.: what about it! You'd better make it good!"

G.B. glanced at Mike's fists clenched by his sides, and dropped wearily on to the low window ledge, his hands hanging limp over his knees.

"I'm sorry, Mike."

Mike seethed.

"Sorry! That's a fat lot of good! Sixteen decent people —in exchange for your miserable hide, I suppose! I've a good mind to tan it off for you!"

"Go ahead: you're probably right."

Mike took a step forward, but G.B.'s dejected attitude stopped him. He didn't even look up.

"Look here, G.B. That sort of thing's not like you. Maybe I was a bit hasty. But surely you knew what you were doing!"

"Yes, I knew."

"Well then, why ever—?" Mike bit his lip. "Look, G.B., I'm sorry I blew up. Knowing you I guess the pressure must have been pretty heavy." He waited, but G.B. said nothing.

Mike studied him narrowly. This wasn't the old, confident G.B. His face was drawn and his shoulders drooped. He looked badly beaten, cowed even—as though he had lost his self-respect. Mike bit his lip again. G.B. had let them down more than badly—but Gregory was a clever devil: he must have got at him somehow. Mike applied his formula for personal tight situations: what might the Lord do in the same place? Justice said G.B. deserved a thrashing, but he'd already had the stuffing knocked out of him somehow. . . .

"O.K., G.B.—let's start again from here!" Mike gave him an encouraging slap on the back.

G.B. looked at him listlessly. "What do you mean?"

"Let's not argue about what's happened: we'll just start from scratch and try and pick up the pieces." Mike held out a hand. "Shake on it?"

A dark flush spread to G.B.'s hair. He stood up hesitantly.

"Thanks, Mike." It was hardly more than a whisper.

He put out his hand, then drew it back suddenly with a sheepish smile. "Er—shall we use the old Scout grip?"

Mike grinned, and they shook left hands.

"Now let's see the other one," said Mike grimly, and before G.B. could stop him he gripped the wrist and opened the curled fingers.

"Oh, no!" Mike was grateful for the toughening effect of his medical training.

G.B. smiled apologetically. "Not awfully pretty, I'm afraid."

Mike gazed horrified at the fiery raw flesh. "But what could make a burn that deep without—?" His eyes narrowed as he remembered the flaked stone. "The burning glass! Was that it? How long did it take, G.B.?" he asked gently.

"Only a second." G.B.'s voice shook. "Honestly, Mike, I couldn't—"

"O.K., O.K.,—no need to put yourself through it again. We've got to get this bound up. Better have a strip of my shirt—another rip or two won't hurt it!"

"Thanks." G.B. smiled ruefully at the neat bandage. "You'll make a doctor yet. What do you want me to do first?"

"For a start—who has the keys to those handcuff things?"

"Huaman had them, but Gregory took them over."

"With most other things, I gather. All right then. You hang around and watch points. Keep as near us as you can. You'll have to take your cue from what happens. I've got to warn the others: if we've got to go through with it we'll have a better chance of holding out if we know what Gregory's got in mind. Good hunting—and watch your step."

"Mike—!"

"Hello?"

"You think it's really important to protect the faith of those people, don't you?"

"Yes, of course!"

"Even though they're only Indians."

"They're Christians—and it's not a case of 'only'."

"I see. Right-ho, Mike: see you later! And—thanks."

Mike aimed a comradely fist at his jaw. "Thank the Lord, not me: it was His idea!"

He peered warily through the curtains, then slipped back the way he had come. He'd have a go at getting hold of those keys later if G.B. didn't manage it, but he'd have to warn the others first. If they knew what was coming it would help them to stick it out—and Mike had a feeling there would be plenty to stick out if Gregory had anything to do with it.

The others agreed with him.

"I think it would help if the Indians knew what was in the air," said Keith. "It would cut a bit of the ground from under his feet." And he translated Mike's words into the dialect.

"The white men tell us that the Great Spirit is stronger than all evil," said the elder calmly when Keith had finished. "We shall rejoice to see that it is so."

"Which doesn't make it any easier!" Mike remarked in English. "I wish they wouldn't look up—"

"Quiet!" Dan hissed.

"Someone coming!" Mike just had time to flatten himself against the wall, his fingers hooked through the two rings as far as they would go, before Gregory came down the steps, followed by some of the priests. At his order the Indians were led away to another part of the crypt out of sight and hearing.

"What are you doing with them!" said Dan.

"I'd rather they didn't hear a proposition I'm about to make to you," said Gregory grimly. "Nor do I want you to translate it to them later."

At that moment Gregory turned away, apparently looking for something on the floor behind him. Mike's nerves thrilled, and slipping his hands free he gathered —and launched in a flying tackle. But somehow he missed. Gregory must have side-stepped, for the next thing Mike knew he was flat on his face with a knee in his back, and his arms twisted up between his shoulder blades.

Gregory clicked his tongue reprovingly.

"Foolish, Brent, foolish. I see you haven't learnt even yet that you can't get the better of me." His eyes gleamed savagely for a second. "No one can get the better of me!

I knew you were free as soon as I came in," he went on in his normal tone. "A helpless man hasn't the bright, tense eyes of the man planning a desperate action."

Mike lay still, seething with anger at himself. Gregory had deliberately turned away, knowing exactly what he would do.

An expert blow to the side of the head half stunned him. With no power to resist he felt the knee taken from his back, and he was lifted to his feet, both wrists held behind in one steel hand. Just as easily he was locked again into the rings on the wall, with a further pair fastened tightly round his ankles.

Gregory folded his arms, smiling confidently, and considered them for a moment, then

"I've a simple proposition for you," he said. "Ah—our good priests return." He waited until the last had gone up the steps. "I've no doubt our Indian friends find some consolation in being reunited with their prince and the others once more," he remarked in English at the last priest's back.

"So Tupac is still alive!" Keith jumped at the information.

Gregory scowled at his careless slip, then shrugged. "What does it matter? Yes, he's alive. The High Priest will deal with him in his own way. Huascar as well—" Gregory cocked an amused eyebrow at a grunt from Mike "—did you guess? But I don't think I shall need him after all. So long as the end is the same the means don't concern me. Which brings me to my proposition again."

"You needn't bother. The answer's No to anything you could propose!" Mike snapped. He was getting a bit fed up with Gregory.

For a moment there was an ugly expression in Gregory's eyes, but a sudden prolonged rumbling put an end to the episode. The floor vibrated through their feet, and a fine shower of dust fell from the roof.

"I don't like the sound of it," Keith muttered. "It's getting worse, I'm sure."

The sound rolled and echoed round the crypt as though trying to find its way out.

"Nor do I," said Gregory. "And after tomorrow—or perhaps even tonight—I shall be on my way home, and well away from it."

"Home! Without the skull!" Mike gaped.

"Indeed not!"

"You mean you've—found it?" Mike couldn't believe it. "But you can't have!"

"So you do know where it is." Gregory nodded his satisfaction, and for the second time Mike could have kicked himself for an ass. "I just wanted to make sure. Now, my proposition. As you can appreciate, it is essential in a self-contained city of this kind that there should be no subversive influences, so—"

"Oh, save your breath," Mike interrupted wearily; "we know all about your grubby proposition."

Gregory's eyes narrowed. "Oh?"

"What do you think I was doing while I was free— playing marbles? Incidentally, we've already translated it to the Indians."

Mike saw another point go up against him on Gregory's scoreboard.

Dan's grave voice broke in. "You're playing a losing game, Gregory. You're fighting God—and you can't win."

Gregory regarded him levelly. "I've managed fairly well until now."

"You'll try Him just a bit too much. He has endless patience, but you'll overstep the mark once too often!"

Gregory's lips curled sneeringly. "Surely He'll have some respect for a clever opponent! And don't you sing about 'gentle Jesus, meek and mild'? I think I'll be able to talk Him round when I meet Him!"

Mike quivered.

"You? You'll be so busy trying to get away from His blinding holiness you won't even be able to open your mouth! When He looks into your messy little soul you'll wish the earth'd open and swallow you out of His sight!"

Mike felt himself actually trembling with fury at this puny creature's miserable defiance. He saw Gregory for the first time as he really was. "We're fed up to the back teeth with you and your miserable ego!" He laughed shakily. "If you weren't tragic you'd be funny! Go on! That's your answer for everything—you haven't the moral backbone even to know what mercy means!"

Gregory had raised a clenched fist, and Mike waited for it to fall. Gregory stood looking at him for a full half minute, his pupils tiny points of black fury, his rigid face dull crimson, then grey-white. Slowly he relaxed, and lowered his arm. He spoke softly, smooth as silk.

"Oh yes, Brent. I know what mercy means. I'm prepared to offer you and your friends a quick end—in exchange for that skull. The High Priest wants a simple denial of 'the God called Jesus' as he puts it, but when you scream for the mercy I offer he'll be satisfied, and the Indians won't know any difference. So you see, Brent," he added, "I win both ways."

"I'll be sorry to disappoint you!"

Gregory smiled. "You won't." He moved towards the steps. "I'm sorry I can't give you longer to make up your mind, but today is to be a great day for Xicchu, I understand, with sacrifices beginning at noon—you, of course, being the first offering. Unless, of course, you wisely decide to save yourself a great deal of discomfort in the meantime. After all, what are a few easily spoken words compared with hours of exquisite agony? And, believe me, 'exquisite' is the word."

He began to mount the steps.

"Gregory!" He turned at Keith's ejaculation. "Gregory —what form are the sacrifices taking?"

"I think they call it 'the Eye of Xicchu'."

Keith's face was unreadable, but as Mike caught Dan's look of horror, his heart thumped with a terrible suspicion.

"And you are offering us all a speedy end in exchange for the skull——?"

"And a few simple words of denial—either literal or implied."

"What happens if you don't get them?"

"The High Priest will carry on in his own way—slowly. But I don't seriously think that will arise."

"And the Indians?"

"Once they have been well disillusioned they'll be turned loose to do their part. They'll be quite useful. A demoralized Christian is even better than no Christian at all."

"You see it as all very easy, don't you, Gregory?" said Keith. "But you're forgetting just one thing—even the weakness of God is stronger than men—and we back that strength against anything you can do."

Gregory looked at Mike, and smiled. "We'll see." He paused again at the top of the steps. "Incidentally, as you know, Oban, I am in my simple way something of a vulcanologist. I give this mountain three days before it blows up and cracks this city right across." He glanced at Mike again. "That is why I'm going to have the skull and be away by tomorrow evening—at the latest."

10

THE EYE OF XICCHU

A SILENCE followed Gregory's exit, and a long, low rumbling from beneath their feet ominously underlined his words.

"I don't doubt he's right," said Keith at last.

But Mike was sweating. "Blow the mountain! What about this 'Eye of Xicchu'! Keith—what is it?"

But even before Keith confirmed his supicions, he knew. A ghastly vision of G.B.'s hand swam in front of him. He fought down a sickening rush of panic.

"T-tricky situation!" He forced his face into a weak grin. Was there a way through this one? He certainly couldn't see it. He gave up trying to put a cheerful face on it. "Dan—what am I going to do!"

Dan looked grim. "Is there any possibility of getting loose again?"

"Mike, the situation's too serious to beat about the head. "Not a hope: he's fastened everything too tight this time. I'll just have to stick it out, that's all."

Keith spoke quietly.

"Mike, the situation's too serious to beat about the bush. I'm going straight through it. No one can stand up to the Eye of Xicchu, however strong he thinks he is. Sooner or later he'll realize the full frightfulness of it, and he'll either lose his reason before it even touches him— which is perhaps the most merciful—or else he'll die by —well, inches. You say you've seen G.B.'s hand. That happened in the early morning in a second. The spot

takes three hours to travel the length of the altar. I'll tell
you quite frankly, Mike, if you weren't a Christian there
would be no problem at all, and no one would dare blame
you for taking the way out. As it is—"

"As it is—I've got to decide just how important it is
not to say a few easy words. Seems crazy, doesn't it?"

"And whether you can lean on the Lord's strength,"
Keith added gently.

But that wasn't very much help. It was well enough
to lean in a reasonably vague way, but when it came to
things like . . . Mike forced the picture out of his mind.
He thought of all the people who had gone through
frightful things simply because they wouldn't say a few
words of the same kind. Was it really worth it? The
Lord knew that he really believed in Him. Surely it
wouldn't matter if he just said them without really meaning them? The Indians didn't really depend on the white
men for their faith. If they really believed in Him it
wouldn't really make any difference, whatever Mike did.
Really. And it would mean it would all be over quickly if
Gregory kept his word. . . .

But what would the Lord think of it all?

Keith said if he weren't a Christian there would be no
problem; but he was, and now the problem was a different
one. He knew perfectly well what he ought to do, what he
wanted to do, but—had he the nerve to do it? The Lord
wouldn't make him do it—the choice was still his own.

For an endless hour his brain tied itself in knots trying
to think of good reasons why he shouldn't go through
with it. But however hard he tried to convince himself
none of the reasons was quite good enough. The others
said nothing, and he was glad: he'd rather be left to work
this out for himself. And he hadn't long to do it now.

He could just see Keith's watch . . . nine o'clock . . .
three hours. Mike closed his eyes. The grisly alternative
came back to him in a vivid rush, and he opened them
again quickly.

The lamps grew dimmer as the minutes—then the quarters—slipped by. Dan and Keith were showing slight signs of strain: there was damp on Keith's forehead. They were involved in this. Only John Akobe stood perfectly still, his chin sunk on his broad black chest, his face like carved ebony.

Mike felt that panic rising again—and this time he couldn't fight it down! He'd always known he'd be no good if it came to it!

Suddenly all his arguments collapsed, and he didn't try to stop them. There just wasn't a good enough reason why he shouldn't go through with it: and he couldn't invent one. He was fighting God, like Gregory, and it had worn him out.

He closed his eyes, and leaned his head wearily against the wall. There was no other answer: he'd have to do it. He was admittedly scared sick. But what else could he do —if Christ really meant anything to him.

Then a hand gripped his shoulder. A hand he couldn't see or feel, but a firm hand that set his nerves humming again, smoothly and coolly this time, like a new engine. A hand that Mike knew was powerful and wouldn't let go. The Lord had been waiting hours for him just to relax and pass over the wheel, and like a scared fool he had been struggling against Him all the time! Mike didn't kid himself the beastly Eye would burn any the less for it, but he knew he hadn't to cope in his own strength—and there was no limit to the strength of the strong Son of God Who held him in such a firm grip.

Mike took a long breath.

Dan looked up anxiously. "O.K., Mike?"

Mike nodded at him. "O.K.!" For a second he wondered how they would react, but a quiet "Thank the Lord!" from Keith set his mind at rest. "How's the time?" he asked.

Keith's watch showed a quarter past eleven, and Mike felt a quick shock. He hadn't realized it was so late! He thought of G.B. Perhaps it was just as well he was out of it: he wouldn't come to much harm. Mike smiled to himself. Poor G.B.! He probably wouldn't understand this at all!

Then a shaft of light shot down the steps as the covering rug was kicked aside. Time was up!

Gregory came down slowly, an anticipatory smile on his face.

"Well, Brent—?" He stopped, apparently put out by Mike's almost cheerful expression.

"Yes, thanks!" Mike couldn't resist it.

Gregory recovered himself at once. "I take it you have some good news for me."

"The best!"

"Ah?"

"If you'd like to feel in my back pocket you'll find it: the Good News according to Matthew, Mark, Luke, and John. It's a bit dog-eared, but you're very welcome."

Gregory shot him a venomous look and gestured sharply to the priests behind him.

The Indians, quiet and calm, were taken through first, then the others. They were unbound, but as usual Gregory was taking no risks with numbers, and Mike could see there was no possibility of escape.

"Tupac and Huascar are safely stowed in a chamber under the altar," said Gregory in answer to Mike's query. "Their appearance would be embarrassing, to say the least, since the High Priest has proclaimed them dead! But Tupac will be able to hear, anyway."

With this encouraging remark Mike was left alone. It seemed an age before anyone came to fetch him, although it was actually less than ten minutes. He was a little surprised to realize that he wasn't really afraid. His palms tingled a bit, but there was no trace of that panic.

At last the priests came. Mike had given up all idea of getting away, and walked quietly through the passages to the temple. He could hear Huaman's voice as they drew near, and the people responding with shouts of "Xicchu!"

The vast, austere temple was crowded. The section of thatch had been taken away, and the sun glared in, focusing on the floor to the left of the altar steps. Mike gave just one quick glance at the stone block. He could see the two groups of prisoners, one on either side of the steps, the priests lined up behind them. He caught a glimpse of G.B. and Gregory half behind a square pillar near Dan's group. And centrally, dominating the whole temple—the writhing, gleaming serpent. In the clean sunlight its evil was, if possible, even more apparent.

They had evidently been making preparations. A row of three herb-filled bowls stood either side of the altar, one to a step. The High Priest was in the act of placing the last bowl with elaborate ceremony. Mike smiled to himself. Huaman was certainly making the most of the occasion: his scarlet-robed figure was almost majestic, and exactly calculated to inspire an appropriate awe. The trouble was, that was just what it did do! He returned to the bottom of the steps and spread his arms in his favourite gesture. The crowd hushed.

"O great Xicchu, who seest all: reveal to us—where is he that defies thee in the name of the strange god?"

With a transparently theatrical—yet effective—air of mystery he turned, and pointed over the heads of the people to the doorway where Mike had been brought.

"There—he is there, the unbeliever! Bring him forth, that Xicchu may look upon him!"

Huaman had clearly prepared his ground well. Hostile faces stared at Mike as the burly priests hustled him forward through the lane opened for them in the crowd. The same crowd who had sung a welcome to them earlier, Mike reflected wryly. As they came to the foot of the steps Mike noticed that Gregory had moved forward to a position nearer the altar.

"Come near, unbeliever!"

Huaman had moved higher and looked down on Mike

with folded arms from the top step. "So this is he who presumes to defy the mighty Xicchu! He who declares his god to be mightier!" Anger buzzed through the packed temple. With another extravagant gesture Huaman stepped aside. "Prepare the sacrifice! We shall see whether his god can save him from the vengeance of Xicchu!"

Mike stiffened and dug in his toes as the priests grasped him and hauled him up the steps. They weren't going to have it all their own way!

"I think the sacrifice is nervous," Gregory murmured in English to no-one in particular.

Mike let go. It wouldn't give a very good impression! The priests stripped off his shirt and were about to take his boots when Gregory intervened.

"I am sure the merciful Xicchu would grant his dying wish, O High Priest: and allow him to keep his boots."

Mike acknowledged the irony with a grim smile.

Huaman turned to Mike. "White man: Xicchu is indeed merciful. If you will acknowledge him he will not take vengeance."

Mike wasn't sure of the Quechua for "Go boil your head", but what he did say apparently conveyed his meaning, judging by the colour of the High Priest's face. His bronze headdress quivering, Huaman flung out his arms again.

"Let the sacrifice begin!"

The priests were at least efficient. They hauled Mike easily on to the stone slab, laying him on his front. Two fastened his wrists to two of the metal rings close together at one end. Another stretched him out while a third pair clamped his ankles. They stepped back and—this was it!

Mike tried to ease his wrists in the metal rings. He was stretched so tightly his ribs scraped on the rough stone. By craning his neck between his arms and looking side-ways he could just see a small angle of the temple. He caught Dan's eye and tried to grin, but couldn't lift his chin high enough for Dan to see. His best view was straight ahead. If he rested his chin on the stone and forced his arms and fingers as far apart as possible—at most four centimetres—he could see the row of bowls on the steps, the spot of light, and G.B. just beyond. Until G.B. moved away.

But it was the light which drew his eyes. If they wandered for a moment they always came back to that imperceptibly moving bright oval on the floor. It was like a magnet, pulling his mind back all the time.

He twisted his head to watch the High Priest, but it made his neck ache too much. The spot mounted the first step and its edges were a little sharper.

He tried to shift his ribs off the hard stone, but he couldn't move enough. He turned his head to the other side and closed his eyes. It was queer how the rumbling travelled through the stone. He wondered what G.B. was thinking, though nothing had actually happened yet. The spot seemed hardly to have moved.

If he weren't so uncomfortable he might easily go to sleep. He felt as though he hadn't slept for years. Huaman had stopped talking; what was he up to now? Mike peered round. Ah, there he was—at the bottom of the steps getting a grandstand view!

A sudden shout from the crowd startled Mike. His mind flew back to the spot. His forehead went cold: the first of the bowls of herbs was smouldering three steps below. A blue flame, almost invisible in the sunlight, flickered across it, and the scent drifted to him on the still air. The beam crept across the bowl and left a dense cloud of blue smoke rising slowly.

Mike found it more difficult not to watch the creeping light. Sometimes it seemed almost to stand still—and then to run at him.

It was coming up to the second bowl—two steps down.

Another millimetre.... The leaves curled and shrivelled at once, and the blue flame licked up. Mike found himself pushing with all his strength against the bands round his wrists. He let go, breathing hard. He'd have to keep a better hold on himself than this. If it got him down at this early stage—!

He must concentrate on the Lord! He was there all right: Mike had known He would be. But He wouldn't make it easy. Mike had known that, too.... He never said He'd make anything easy....

Mike's eyes slid back to the spot on the second step: it was less oval now, and much sharper at the edges.

There was a constant low murmuring from the body of the temple. Of all those he could see, only Gregory seemed unmoved. He stood easily, with thumbs hooked in his belt, a ghost of a smile on his face.

Mike rested his forehead on the cool stone. It wouldn't be long now. He could feel his heart beating high up, almost in his throat. He forced himself to relax—and immediately began to tighten up again. He made himself keep his head down, and drove his thoughts back.

His hands were getting stiff.... He'd once heard a sermon about the Lord's hands ... he always imagined He must have had a mighty strong grip ... he must concentrate—concentrate!

The crowd was quiet. Mike raised his head. His heart pounded uncontrollably. The brilliant gold spot, almost round, had reached the top step. He stared at it, remorselessly moving on. It reached the edge of the bowl—and slipped in. The leaves exploded in a brilliant orange and blue flare, almost in his eyes! He flinched back, burying his streaming face between his arms—trying to hide—to get away from that terrible light that nothing could stop. He lay gasping, his throat rigid, the shouts deafening him. The fever was taking hold of them again.

It was all right—he drew a quivering breath: the Lord wouldn't leave go of him. Mike controlled his shaking and set his lips hard together.

He couldn't see the light now: it was below his line of vision on the top step. He glanced at Huaman. He was swaying slightly forward, arms tightly folded, his eyes bright. The fever was gripping him, too, in reality this time.

The people had grown quiet again. All eyes were fixed at the same point.

Way down below him Mike heard the mountain rolling again. A deep, threatening roll, surging up from the depths of the earth, and vibrating through the stone into his chest. Well, he needn't worry about that! By the time it blew up—if it was going to!—he'd be——

He froze. A tiny arc of light was creeping over the edge of the block, ten centimetres from his fingers. Paralyzed, he watched it gradually become an almost perfect circle.

Eight centimetres.... The atmosphere was electric.

Six centimetres.... Some dust particles sizzled and smoked for an instant. His mouth was drying up and he could hardly breathe.

Four centimetres....

Instinctively he pulled his fingers back.

Two centimetres.... He couldn't get them back any farther.... If he pressed back hard enough the spot would pass between his hands—but it would just catch the wrist clamps. He stared at them and couldn't see them. He wiped his eyes on his arm. What were they made of?—perhaps it wouldn't conduct——

The light touched.

It seemed an eternity before the spot slipped off on to the stone again. A perfect circle now, the size of a ten-penny piece, it beat down with a white heat, scorching the hairs on Mike's arms on either side of it. He dragged his arms as far apart as he could, straining away—giving himself as long as he could before—. His heart bumped suddenly with a kind of exultation. He hadn't given in—and he wasn't going to! The Lord was nearer to him than any of those savages could possibly understand. Perhaps nearer than even Dan or Keith could understand. God gave His strength when we needed it and not before—and they didn't need it quite so much as he did at that moment!

But the real testing point was still to come. He knew that. And it would be too much for him on his own.

The hairs were singed now from wrist to elbow. He tried to lift his head ... but he was curiously weak. It was right in the path of the light, and he could do absolutely nothing about it. He closed his eyes wearily. Oh well, another two inches and he would be either crazy or beyond caring. He didn't mind dying—it was only a doorway, and the Lord would be on the other side of it. ... He hoped it would happen quickly ... he didn't want to lose his mind ... it was wandering already ... people singing—crazy idea ... thunder rocking the place— lightning ... a horrible smell of singeing hair ... singing —singing—singing—like a hymn ... funny tune ... louder than all the other rumpus ... the Christians— singing ... trust them! ... awful pain in the head— somebody shouting—rocking the boat—making a terrible row ... noisy enough anway—roaring and rumbling.... Xicchu, what's happening to Xicchu.... He twisted his head sideways with a last great effort.

With a tearing, splitting crack the gleaming monster swayed off balance. Slowly it leaned forward, and slowly the evil, top-heavy head bore down on the crowd. With screams of panic they rushed out of its path, and out of the rocking building. Huaman stood staring up at it, apparently unable to believe his eyes. Mike suddenly came to his senses. The great shadow of the monster had cut off the white-hot beam!

"Look out!" he croaked. But his voice didn't carry above the pandemonium. The thing crashed across him on to the stone floor. It balanced for a second on its bent head, then its neck broke, and it collapsed with a sudden jerk.

Mike shut his eyes quickly. The High Priest had stared a second too long.

11

"I NEVER MISS!"

MIKE couldn't see what was happening. The shouting
and crashing deafened him: the ground rocked. The
priests scattered and for a minute Mike thought he was
alone. The great mass of the serpent lying down the steps
blocked his sight—and it was growing dark. A pillar
further down the temple fell with a crash—then another.
Then a hand—a flesh and blood hand—was hot on his
back.

"Mike! Are you all right!"

Mike grinned feebly. "Hello, Dan. Yes, all O.K. Can
you get me out of these?"

Dan called across the steps. "Bring him here."

Keith and John Akobe, balancing themselves on the
rocking floor, hauled Gregory up the steps.

"How do you open these things—who has the key?"

"I don't know—either!"

"John Akobe—we've got to get out of here at once—
do you think you could do it?"

The massive black hands gripped one of the wrist
clamps. Slowly the metal buckled under the iron fingers.

With a grunt John Akobe snapped the catch.

"Thanks, John Akobe!" Mike eased his hand out while
John Akobe set to work on the others. His wrists were only
slightly scorched from the hot metal, but he was as stiff
as a post. He could hardly force his arms down. Keith
massaged some life into them, while Mike sent up silent
and very hearty thanks.

The Indians were all still standing in the same place,

not seeming to know what to do or what was happening.

Another violent upheaval beneath their feet sent them all slithering to one side.

"Quick, let's get out of here!"

Dan shouted terse orders to the Indians, and all made for the temple door, staggering crazily. Before they could reach it the end wall collapsed, and with it part of the heavy thatch, completely blocking their way. They came to a sudden halt, and Dan's mouth tightened.

"Right—the side door!"

Another shock blocked the remaining exit.

"Only one thing for it—we'll have to go below!" Dan roared above the din. "We can't get out this way—and the roof's going to collapse any minute!"

Mike suddenly remembered. "Tupac! We've forgotten Tupac! He's under the altar somewhere! And Huascar!"

"You're right!" shouted Dan as they hurried back down the temple. "Good—Tupac knows the passages— he'll be able to get us out!"

John Akobe ripped Tupac's rings out of the wall, and hoisted the still unconscious Huascar across his shoulders like a doll.

"There is another door—behind the altar!" said Tupac. "Quickly!"

He was halfway up the steps when a violent quake almost threw him off his feet. There was a deafening crash overhead, and the light was cut off.

"We've had it that way!" Mike shouted, bracing himself against the wall.

The mountain seemed to exhaust itself with this last violent effort, and gradually the noise and shaking subsided.

"It's only gathering its strength to get going again!" said Dan grimly. "Tupac, can you lead us out?"

"Yes, there are ways."

"Good. Wait a minute: is anyone hurt or missing?"

"G.B.! What about G.B.? I haven't seen him." Mike looked round the group.

"I'm—I'm here," G.B. spoke hesitantly from the back.

"We'll have to put it to everyone," said Dan gravely. "Do you all agree to this man's coming with us?"

Comac spoke for the Indians. "Is the heart of the white man full of sorrow for his deed?"

Mike looked sideways at G.B. It wasn't exactly G.B.'s language, but Mike guessed Comac had hit it pretty well on the head.

G.B. nodded. "Yes." His lack of embarrassment surprised Mike. He must really mean it.

"Then we are glad. He must come." Comac smiled.

Everyone looked at Gregory.

"How do you suggest stopping me?" he sneered.

"Hands and feet are easily tied!" said Keith.

"I see—Christians don't mind indirect murder then!"

"He's right," said Dan. "We couldn't leave him here. It seems it's our hands that are tied." He looked at Comac.

"The Great Spirit is just," the little Indian said enigmatically.

Gregory narrowed his eyes. "Meaning?"

"He will judge in His own time. It matters not whether it be early or late, the evil man shall not escape His judgment."

Mike had a fleeting vision of the High Priest as he had last seen him.

"If it's late enough He may forget all about it!" Gregory sneered. "Lead on, Tupac, and get us out of this tomb!"

They set off, Tupac and Keith leading, the Indians following, and Mike and the others bringing up the rear. Gregory, with contemptuous confidence, varied his position, sometimes following behind, sometimes walking with the leaders.

"Which way are you going, Tupac?" Dan called after five minutes of hurrying through passages.

"To the sacred pool."

"We hope!" Mike muttered.

Tupac led them swiftly through the passages, only to come to a sudden stop.

"Blocked!" Mike's exclamation was unnecessary.

"There is also a way to the High Priest's chambers in the temple."

They hurried after Tupac in the opposite direction, only to pull up short in the face of another wall of rubble. They all looked at Tupac.

"There is another way—" He hesitated as the mountain began to growl again, faint and menacing.

"Yes?" said Dan.

"But it leads through the mountain."

"*Through* the mountain!" Mike's heart missed a beat.

"I'm afraid we've no option," said Dan. "It's a nasty risk, but staying here would be a nastier certainty."

They set off again through a maze of passages. Tupac seemed to be following some directions or other, although Mike couldn't see any sign at all. The lamps were fewer now, and Tupac took one from a niche as he passed. There was an absolute silence all round except for the low threatening rumble of the mountain. They were walking into the depths of the earth.

The passages began to have a vaguely familiar look to Mike. They had come to the living rock. Yes—there it was!

"There it is, Dan!" Mike pointed up at the snake over the entrance to the passage as they passed. "Where I——!"

Mike almost ground his teeth. Why couldn't he keep his mouth shut! But Gregory, walking ahead, gave no sign of having heard.

It was getting warmer in the passage, but Mike didn't think it accounted for the rate of G.B.'s breathing.

"He ought to be shot!" G.B. suddenly muttered.

Mike started at the venom in G.B.'s voice. He'd better head this off a bit!

"What's the charge?" he said lightly. "You can't

execute a man just for being a nasty bit of work, even if he is about the limit."

"Oh?" There was no lightness in G.B.'s tone. It was cold, and unnaturally hard. "He's going to pay for what he did to us."

Mike felt uneasy. This wasn't like G.B. He studied him from the corner of his eye. G.B. was flushed, and his eyes curiously bright. And where even the Indians were oozing with moisture his skin was perfectly dry. Something was wrong.

"Don't talk like an idiot!"

G.B. smiled, a calm smile. "I'm in no hurry." His hand brushed his pocket. "We can wait."

Mike thought furiously. He contrived to bump G.B. after a minute or two: there was no doubt about it. G.B. had managed to get hold of the revolver again somehow. But he wasn't normal.

"Better let me have it, G.B.," said Mike casually.

G.B.'s eyes blazed with suspicion. "Why?"

"Oh nothing. It doesn't matter."

He would have to keep an eye on him. Gregory might be the limit, but it would still be murder to shoot him down. They were walking last: it was too close quarters to have a private word with Dan or John Akobe. If G.B. were excited in any way he might go off the rails altogether. And Mike didn't dare risk taking his eyes off him.

It was getting warmer. The rumbling was still quiet, but more insistent.

Dan went forward to have a word with Tupac, and reported back.

"Tupac says it's not far now. We've come a kilometre at least. I gather the passage comes out above the forest on the opposite side to where we came in. As far as I can translate his timing another half an hour should see us through."

When Dan had fallen in beside John Akobe again Mike saw G.B.'s hand slide to his pocket. He tensed, but G.B.

only felt inside, and smiled to himself. He seemed oblivious of Mike altogether.

He was clearly not in his right mind. Mike had to get that revolver away from him or G.B. would do something he'd be sorry for! He tried a direct approach.

"You realize it'll be murder," he said in a low voice.

"Justice."

"Who are you to judge and sentence?"

G.B. held out his hand. "He's going to pay for what he did to me."

"Aren't you forgetting something?"

"He's going to pay for what he did to you as well."

"But I don't want his life for that."

"I do."

"Look here, G.B.—" Mike began soothingly.

G.B. suddenly turned feverishly bright eyes on him.

"I suppose you'd forgive him," he sneered, "and let bygones be bygones!"

Mike flushed. "I'd forgive him, yes, for what he'd done to me, if he was interested."

G.B. sneered again. "That's a good little Christian— love your enemies! Forgive them: it's an easy way of saving yourself the risk of paying them out! Well, I'm not taking any easy way out! He's going to pay for all the rotten things in his rotten soul!"

Mike didn't argue: you couldn't reason with a sick mind.

The air was growing hotter, and Mike was conscious of a faint but unpleasant smell. He knew the smell from Chemistry Lab. games with sulphuric acid and iron filings!

"Must be a vent somewhere in one of the passages," Dan remarked. "But so long as the opening the other end is clear the air should stay breathable."

The rumbling grew noticeably louder.

"Working itself up again," said Dan grimly. "Let's hope it can wait till we're out!"

As if to mock him, the floor heaved, sending them all

sliding against the wall. A shower of grit and dust covered them, getting into eyes and noses. The dust stuck to Mike's damp skin, giving him a grey shirt, and scratching him where he tried to brush it off.

The rumbling rolled angrily.

"I'll find out if Tupac can go any faster," said Dan quietly; "though I don't imagine he needs any urging. I don't want to frighten the others, but it sounds like the beginning of the end to me." He returned after an apparently casual conversation with Tupac. "He's going as fast as he can: but he's picking up some signs on the wall. Blowed if I can see what they are!"

But Mike couldn't look for signs. It took him all his time to keep an eye on G.B. and Gregory. Gregory had fallen into an apparently congenial position close behind Tupac and Keith, in front.

There was an almost continuous roaring deep under their feet now, and the air was stuffily warm. The Indians stumbled wearily on, and Mike found the events of the last few days had taken a heavy toll of his own stamina.

Dan ran a hand round the back of his collar. "The air's still clean—heat must be coming through the rock," he panted.

John Akobe's skin shone like varnished ebony. Only G.B. seemed unaffected. He strode along, arms by his sides, his hands and face perfectly dry. Mike judged it as some kind of nervous shock, and hardly wondered. But he had to get that revolver somehow! Once G.B. got out of the tunnel there was no knowing what might happen.

Dan bent and felt the stone floor. "Thought so. Getting warmer," he muttered to Mike. "It's—hold on!"

A roar like an express train deafened them. The whole passage lurched, throwing them in a struggling heap on the floor.

"Too near to be healthy!" Dan bellowed as they picked themselves up. "Probably breaking through underneath by degrees!"

Mike's head ached with the earsplitting din. The

ground was uncomfortably hot, even through leather boots.

"Shouldn't be much further!" Dan shouted at the top of his voice. Tupac waved an arm. "Good—Tupac's signal—almost there!"

Mike nodded and shouted back. "Much more of this and you can have my eardrums for fourpence!"

Suddenly the noise abated—so suddenly that they were startled. Then, from a long way away, it growled up from the depths of the earth, shaking down lumps of the roof, roaring up at them—nearer every second. Mike clapped his hands over his ears and ducked. Dan's fingers dug into his arm.

"Where's it coming through?"

A noise like a hundred tons of T.N.T. hit Mike like a physical force: a blast of searing, thick air enveloped him. There was a yell of "Back!" from somewhere, and Mike found himself scrambling along the way they had come— running, tripping, half picking himself up again, scrambling along on hands and knees—all the time smothered by that thick, fearful-smelling cloud.

"Ease up—far enough!" Keith called a halt at last. Mike looked back. Not a hundred metres on from where they had been, a glowing split in the ground was throwing up gouts of blood-red lava. They smacked against the roof and fell back on to the floor, spreading sluggishly like red dough, cooling to a greyish-white lump. Some stuck to the roof and dripped slowly, like some horrible stalactite. Mike shuddered.

The atmosphere was stifling, though breathable again. Their council was held in brief shouts above the deafening roar of the underground furnace.

"Way blocked!" Keith shouted; "Can't go on! Another way, Tupac?"

Tupac held up one finger.

"Right—lead on!"

Trying to keep their balance on the quaking floor they hurried further back. Tupac turned off to the left.

Mike's heart gave one thump, and died. The passage was a mass of rubble from roof to ceiling.

The Indians crowded round, looking helplessly from one to another of the white men. Gregory scowled at the blocked way.

"What now?" said Dan. The noise was lessening slightly. "Is this the only way left, Tupac?"

Tupac nodded again. "The other ways do not lead anywhere."

"Then there's only one thing for it." Everyone looked at Keith. "We'll have to cross that fissure."

Some of the Indians gave a faint cry of fear, and Mike could hardly believe his ears. Keith held up a hand. "Listen. The mountain is quietening down again. This may be our last chance before it really blows up. I'll go and reconnoitre. John Akobe, leave Huascar here and come with me. The others come as far as is obviously safe. Gregory, you come with me as well. You know something about this sort of thing."

G.B. made as though to go after Gregory as he followed the other two towards the still glowing crack.

"It's O.K., G.B.," Mike said gently, catching his sleeve. "He can't go far."

G.B. seemed satisfied, and came back docilely, but his staring eyes didn't leave Gregory for a moment.

The three made their inspection while the others watched from a safe distance. The spurts of lava were far less frequent now, and a darker red. They rarely reached the roof, and simply fell back into the crack, catching on the edges and hanging there.

"Can't be very wide," said Mike hopefully. Dan nodded silently.

The three returned, their faces puffy with the heat.

"Quietening down fast," said Keith. "Gregory estimates from fifteen minutes to half an hour, then it should be quiet enough. I agree with him, as far as I can tell. I think we can take his word on it. The fissure itself is only half a metre wide so there's no difficulty there. I suggest John Akobe and I go first: Dan, Mike and G.B. stay this side and help the others across to us."

The Indians were clearly apprehensive, and Mike wasn't sorry when the half-hour was up.

"It hasn't spouted for fifteen minutes," said Keith. "Come on now, as quickly as you can."

The heat roasted them as they neared the crack.

"Must be hundreds of degrees!" gasped Mike. Dan turned a streaming face to him.

"About a thousand right down there at the bottom."

Mike looked over the edge where Dan pointed. The walls fell away sheer for many metres, only broken by a ledge or a crack here and there. Grey at the top, they changed from dark red to vermilion as they widened out near boiling lava three hundred metres down. The molten rock seethed and bubbled with a deafening roar, bursting in great craters and letting out clouds of foul-smelling gases and steam. A white-hot spout leaped thirty metres into the air. It fell and was swallowed up at once in the churning, viscous mass below.

"Here goes!"

Keith stepped quickly over the crack, and John Akobe and his burden followed. Tupac went next, then recrossed and waited until all the Indians had gone over. Even under those conditions Mike found time to be impressed by Tupac's behaviour: he was a chief in the making.

"You next, G.B.—Gregory—Mike."

Dan came last.

With a protesting rumble fifteen centimetres of the rock edge broke off and plunged down into the inferno.

"Full speed ahead, Tupac!"

They set off, putting as much distance as possible between them and that voracious pit. Gregory apparently changed his mind and walked behind. This seemed to satisfy G.B. and he walked on without turning round. Mike studied him: he was planning something. But so long as Gregory was behind them G.B. couldn't do much.

The air grew rapidly cleaner. Comac was the first to see the shaft of daylight from the opening, and then it was an undignified race. They collapsed, laughing and slapping one another on the back, on a flat sunbaked shelf of rock overlooking the forest.

"Right!" said Dan cheerfully but briskly. "On your feet everyone. We're still too near to be comfortable." He squinted over the dense trees, shading his eyes against the brilliant afternoon light. "We'd better make for the nearest river." He pointed to a distinct curving line of brighter green half a kilometre to the right. "That one will do."

Tupac got up slowly and stood beside him.

"But—our people?"

"I'm sorry, Tupac," said Keith gently: "there's nothing you can do now. It would mean crossing the mountain to get to the city. They will have gone up into the mountains on the other side: they'll be safe there. As soon as it's possible you can go to them. It will do no good if you try to cross the mountain and it blows you to pieces, will it?"

Tupac nodded in his dignified way. "Brother Keith speaks wise words, as always." And he rejoined the group of Indians standing quietly on the far side of the shelf.

"We might be able to fly him in—or at least land him reasonably near," Dan observed to Keith in English.

"Better get moving," said Mike, joining the others on the edge. "Nobody's missing. We were at the back so we'd have seen anyone drop out."

Mike's palms tingled. No—they weren't at the back! Gregory was the last—and where was Gregory?

"He didn't pass us when we came out," said Keith.

Mike shot a horrified look at G.B.

"He stayed behind," said G.B., with a sloping smile.

"G.B.—you didn't—!" Mike ran to the tunnel entrance and peered in.

"Oh no— he went back soon after we crossed the vent."

"The crass idiot! He'll never find his way out!" Dan

joined Mike at the opening. He rounded on G.B. "Why didn't you say something—you knew he'd never find his way out again!"

"Yes," said G.B. calmly, hands in his pockets.

Dan stared speechlessly at him. Mike caught his arm. "Hold on, Dan," he muttered. "I think he's gone a bit queer in the head or something."

Dan relaxed, looking keenly at G.B. They moved back to the others. "I think you're right, Mike. Accumulation of shock, I should say." He raised his voice to normal. "Well, there's nothing we can do about Gregory now. We'd better go while the going's good."

"Are we going to leave him to it?"

"Can't do much else," said Dan. "He's obviously gone back for the skull. He may have estimated he'd have enough time, but I'm afraid he won't get out again. He'll never pick the right route unless he has the key."

There was a long silence while they looked at one another.

"All right," said Dan at last, with a rueful grin; "which one goes back for him?"

"Goes back!" G.B. shrieked, He waved his arms wildly. "Go back for that murderer!" He dropped into a snarling sarcasm. "Yes—go back for him! Bring him out safely and let him loose with the skull! That's what we've been working for all this time—and suffering for!" His words choked off in a sob of fury.

"Take it easy, G.B.," said Dan. "You wouldn't want anyone to be buried alive in there."

G.B.'s eyes glinted. "Wouldn't I?"

"You can't argue with him, Dan," said Mike. "Look—it would only need one of you to wait for him at the entrance here—"

"'You'?" Dan repeated.

Mike grinned sheepishly. "Well, I think I've got the best claim to him—if Tupac will give me the directions."

G.B. almost spat in his contempt. "Christian mentality! You're all crazy fools!"

Tupac took Mike to the entrance and pointed to a triangular mark in the stone at eye level on the wall.

"In the true way these point—so." He demonstrated a triangle with his hands. "In all the other ways they point —so—or so."

Mike peered at the mark. "Right. I think I've got it."

"You'd better have it," Dan grunted. "Your skin is going to depend on it! Now—who's going to stay? Keith, the Indians need you. G.B.'s not in favour anyway. So it's you or me, John Akobe."

"'When fighting the lion, the elephant is more to be favoured than the zebra, be the zebra never so courageous'," John Akobe smiled.

"John Akobe's right," said Mike. "Strength will count against Gregory. Then that's settled. Thanks, Dan, but services not required!"

Dan clapped Mike on the shoulder. "Right-ho, Mike. We'll take Huascar and wait for you at the first suitable place on the right bank of the river. We'll make a cairn to guide you, and keep a watch."

"Er—I shouldn't wait longer than a couple of days after you arrive," said Mike. "This job shouldn't take long, of course, and—well, you never know!"

Dan gave him an affectionate shove towards the entrance.

"So long, Mike. Go carefully."

Mike raised his hand to the others. "O.K., John Akobe, here goes. If you hear anything beginning to happen, don't bother to wait for it, will you!"

He turned towards the dark opening.

"Just a moment." G.B. sounded almost sane again, and Mike looked back hopefully.

He found himself staring down a revolver levelled steadily at his head.

"The first man to set a foot in that passage gets a bullet in his brain," said G.B. calmly; "and you know I never miss, Mike."

12

MIKE TAKES HIS OWN BACK

G.B. wasn't joking. His eyes were as steady as his hand, and cold as steel.

"I don't want to kill you, Mike, but I will, rather than let you do anything to help that devil escape what he deserves."

"If you kill me that will be two lives on your hands," said Mike quietly. "G.B., don't be an ass. Put that revolver down and be your age! We're not playing games."

"I know that." The revolver didn't waver.

Mike glanced at the others. No one was in a position to do anything; G.B. had them all covered. He'd have to talk him out of it—and soon. If Gregory got too far lost in those passages he might never find him—at least, not before it was too late to get out again. A growling rumble spurred him on. He looked at G.B. shrewdly. Just how crazed was he? How much of the old G.B. could he work on? He stuck clammy hands in his pockets and spoke as calmly as he could.

"Look here, G.B.: you're not the sort to go around shooting people down in cold blood!" He snorted. "In any case, I thought you were a pal of mine!"

One of G.B.'s lids flickered. But which had affected him—the "cold blood" or the "friend" angle? In these unbalanced minds small things could weigh heavily. Mike tried again.

"Cold-booded killers are all pretty low types, I find."

"There are exceptions." G.B. was untouched.

"But I don't know of any others who could shoot their pals down."

G.B. said nothing. Mike took a long breath.

"There's one thing about G.B.—I could always trust him not to play any grubby tricks. He'd never do anything behind anybody's back. In fact, I don't think he could stab a chap in the back if he tried. I could always turn my back on him—" he did so, slowly and casually, "—and know I was absolutely safe." Heart thumping desperately, he took a step towards the tunnel. There was dead silence. He took another step. "What would I have to worry about?" he remarked as though to himself: "G.B. would never stab anyone in the back, let alone a pal!" He must keep G.B.'s mind off that revolver in his hand! He reached the tunnel entrance—then his nerve cracked. He dived inside, flinging himself flat on his face.

The bullets smacked against the stone wall and ricocheted over his head. There was the noise of a brief scuffle.

"All right, Mike!" called Dan. "All over!"

Mike wiped his face with his hand, and stepped out into the open again.

"Thanks, Dan!" he gasped. "Is he all right?" G.B. lay on the ground apparently unconscious.

"I think so, I tackled him and he blacked out. Best thing probably. We'll keep an eye on him."

"Right-ho. Tell him—tell him it's O.K. by me, when he really comes round, if he remembers anything."

"Tell him yourself!" Dan grinned at him. "Good hunting, Mike!"

With a nod to John Akobe Mike re-entered the tunnel. It had been bad enough when he was surrounded by people, but the dim, empty silence of these age-old passages, with only the distant rumbling of the furnace for company, was, to say the least, wearing on the nerves. Mike had wondered whether he had any left, but he found some when he turned the corner, and the daylight disappeared, giving place to a red glow. The lamp had spilled and gone out in the rush, so the glow was all he would have to see by.

The triangles here were fairly clear, once you knew where to look. The mountain was certainly lying doggo at the moment: Mike relied on Gregory's apparent knowledge of these things. Gregory wouldn't have gone back if he'd thought he'd be in any danger.

The vent would be about a hundred metres from the bend—ah, yes, there it was, casting its red light on the roof. Good, it was still quiet; but Mike wasn't taking any chances. He took a good run up, and leapt as far as he could. He looked back. Was it a little wider, or did it just seem so?

How far had Gregory got? Best thing would be to see if he'd taken the skull first.

Mike ran down the passage. It seemed fairly straightforward with fewer forks and side passages than he had thought. His footsteps echoing above the muttering and vibrating rock sounded like ghosts running away all round him.

Yes—the skull had gone. So that meant Gregory was lost, or Mike would have met him. He turned to come out—and stopped suddenly.

Passages led off in all directions!

Mike's brain whirled with bewilderment. They hadn't been there when he came in! Then he realized all the entrances faced him! In the dim light they couldn't be seen from the other side because of the angle at which they joined the original passage. You could wipe out an army in a place like this if they tried to turn back!

An irritable snarl and shudder from below jerked Mike back to actualities.

Which passage had Gregory taken? It was no use going down any of them or they'd both be in the same boat. Mike peered at the wall. Triangles pointed all over the place now. Ah—there was the guide mark: not easy to see among all the others.

He cupped his mouth and shouted.

"Gregory!"

"Greg-greg-greg-ry-y-y!" The echo bounced away into unknown empty distances. Mike shivered.

He tried again on the opposite side.

"Gregory! Where are you!"

"Are-you-u-u!"

So he must have struck the right way for a time at least. Mike hurried back, calling down each branch as he came to it. At last, there was a faint response—or was it just an echo? It was difficult to be sure. The mountain was beginning to sound nasty again, and made listening difficult. Mike shouted again, straining his ears for the reply. It came, nearer this time.

"Gregory—follow my voice! You'll never get out from where you are!" The reply was indistinguishable, but obviously derisive.

"I tell you there's only one way out!" Mike bellowed. "You know as well as I do this thing's going to blow up soon. You'll have to take my word or be blown up with it! D'you hear?"

The reply was much nearer this time and heavily sarcastic.

"Why should I take your word for it! Don't tell me you've come to show me the way out!"

"All right—I won't tell you! It's up to you!" The roaring was too loud to be healthy. Mike stuck it for two minutes, then he shouted again. "How long do you think you've got, Gregory?"

There was no reply. A gust of hot gas rushed past making Mike choke and gasp for breath.

He staggered into the tunnel mouth. "Gregory! this is your last chance—are you coming!"

There was a brief pause. Then a figure appeared at the end of the passage. It stopped halfway.

"Why should you come and fetch me out?" he sneered. "It would be to your advantage to leave me here!"

"No doubt," said Mike tersely: "but that's something

you wouldn't understand." He turned away. "Come on, there's no time for polite conversation."

Something pricked his back.

"Just to make sure we don't play any tricks," Gregory breathed in his ear.

"Don't be more of an ass than you have to!" Mike snapped. "You'll never get out without me!"

Gregory apparently saw the wisdom of that, and the point was withdrawn.

A sudden prolonged rolling startled them both.

"Come on!" Mike started off at a run. But the triangles were difficult to distinguish in the mist of falling dust. The noise was becoming deafening again. Mike glanced at Gregory anxiously.

"It's building up faster than I expected." Gregory shouted. "Can't you go any quicker!"

Mike shook his head. "Can hardly see!" he shouted back.

A large rock crashed from the roof just ahead. They jumped back just in time: a hissing jet of scalding steam rushed up from a crack in the floor.

They flattened themselves against the wall, backing away.

"Come on!" Mike shouted as soon as the jet lessened. The dense white cloud blotted everything out. "How long have we got, Gregory?"

"An hour at the outside."

"Should be enough. Hang on to my belt—can't see a thing!"

As soon as the air was cool enough Mike peered his way along the wall. It was slow going, but it shouldn't take them more than half an hour to get out, even at that rate.

An ominous rumble not far ahead and somewhere to the side brought them up short.

"One of the passages fallen in!" Gregory shouted. "Get a move on!"

The steam weighted down the dust, and the air was cleaner, but it was like walking in a Turkish bath.

"We're almost to the vent!" Mike shouted.

"Are you sure!"

"Yes! You can see the glow on the roof! About a hundred metres!"

Then something hit him on the back of the head. . . .

He came to with a tremendous rushing in his ears. He shook the dizziness out of his eyes and levered himself up. An avalanche of rock poured from the roof into the passage twenty metres ahead. He was just in time to see Gregory go down under it.

The deadly rain stopped, and Mike lurched along the passage to the heap of rock. There was no sign of Gregory.

He pulled away some of the loose stones at the bottom. Gregory's three fingers lay quite still clutching the floor. Mike felt for the pulse. It was still active—Gregory was still alive.

Mike began to tear at the rocks—then he suddenly stopped. An hour at the outside: there was hardly that now! It would take him at least fifteen ninutes to get Gregory out. They'd never get clear in time. The fire was boiling and roaring beneath them, gathering strength to come tearing up through the puny rocks that tried to stop it.

Mike jumped up. He'd have to leave Gregory. No one could blame him—it was every man for himself when things got as close as this! No one could blame him. The Lord couldn't blame him either. Besides—Mike's eyes stung with new anger—it must have been Gregory who tried to knock him out! He knew he was near the exit and had got rid of Mike to give himself a clear path! Gregory hadn't thought twice about leaving *him* to be blown to bits! No—he'd let him get on with it this time. And the world in general would be better off without him! He was unconscious, so he wouldn't know anything about it.

With that encouraging thought Mike set off along the rumbling passage, steadying himself against the wall. The

roaring of the fire seemed just underneath his feet. The
rock was almost too hot to walk on.

No—the Lord wouldn't blame him! Mike told himself
again. He didn't expect a bloke to risk chucking his life
away for a blighter like that!

But Christ had thrown His own life away for him. . . .

Mike stopped suddenly. He looked at the fiery red glow
on the roof over the vent. No—the Lord didn't ask that
much of anybody! In any case—there wasn't time!

But He did ask just that much, and Mike knew it.

The stones seemed to weigh a ton, and the sweat dripped off Mike. It seemed centuries before he had uncovered
Gregory's head and shoulders. He gripped him under the
arms and dragged him free.

Gregory was still right out, and gave no sign of coming
round. A blackening bruise on his temple showed why.
There was nothing for it but to drag him along—though
what was going to happen when they reached the vent
remained to be seen!

The mountain was obviously working up to a mighty
explosion of some kind. Mike panted along in a near
panic, dragging a dead weight. The vent was still comparatively quiet and Mike laid Gregory down at a safe
distance while he went to have a closer look.

It had widened to more than three metres.

Mike stared at it, unable to believe his senses.

No—! It would take an Olympic champion to jump
that in these conditions! He stared round desperately for
some means of getting across.

There was a movement in the thick smoke-laden air of
the far side.

"Young Mike—is it you!" boomed John Akobe.

Mike had never seen anything more perfect than the
black, dusty figure which loomed up beyond the gulf.

"Yes—it's me!" he yelled back. "Think of some way to
get across, John Akobe! And quickly!"

"Stand back, young Mike!"

Mike did as he was told, and a liana, thick and strong as

a steel cable, snaked across to him. "A rope bridge!" he breathed. "Good old John Akobe! Right—I've got it!" he shouted.

Gregory was still lying where Mike had laid him, and the effects of the crack on the head were wearing off. He opened his eyes and gazed blearily at Mike.

Suddenly Mike remembered the skull. But Gregory saw his eyes flick to the bulge in his pocket, and grabbed Mike's wrist.

"No you don't!" he snarled.

Then Mike did something he'd never done or thought he would ever do to a man lying almost helpless on his back. He slapped Gregory hard across the mouth with the back of his hand. Gregory let go.

"Get up!" Mike snapped. "We're going over the vent. Go and look at it!"

Gregory glanced at him in the ruddy light, but there was something in Mike's tone which didn't allow for argument. He went and looked at the gaping fissure.

"How?" he shouted.

Mike showed him the rope. "John Akobe's on the other side."

Mike looked round for some means of fastening the end.

"All right," he shouted at last above the mounting noise: "we'll have to hold the ends fast while you swing yourself across by your hands. John Akobe, there's no means of fastening it this side! Gregory's going to swing across—ready?"

"I am ready!" boomed back at Mike.

"And when I'm halfway across you drop your end!" Gregory sneered. "No, thank—!" Suddenly his eyes narrowed. He seemed to be doing some quick calculating. "All right—I'll risk it."

Mike tied the liana firmly round his waist and walked back five metres to the end of it. He lay down and braced himself behind a ridge in the wall.

"Go steadily, Gregory, or you'll have us both in. There's some hold here, but not much. Ready now."

Mike admired Gregory's nerve as he slipped over the edge, to hang in space over that boiling cauldron. Mike braced himself against the first shock, and after that Gregory went across smoothly. Mike could just see his hands moving along the taut rope. He was almost to the other side when there was a sudden jerk, and one of the hands disappeared.

Mike's heart leapt into his mouth. Gregory had slipped! No—he'd got his grip again. What was the idiot doing! He was jerking at the rope almost as though he were doing it deliberately! A regular, bouncing jerk.

"What're you doing!" Mike tried to shout, but couldn't get enough breath in his lying-down position.

Another jerk nearly dislodged him from his ridge. He'd have them both in if he kept it up!

He did keep it up. Mike couldn't hold on any longer— and he was being pulled towards the vent with each jerk! He tried to pull back, but there were no toeholds in the smooth floor. He tried to scramble up but was jerked down again. Mike struggled with the knot at his waist— Gregory was so near the other edge that John Akobe could easily pull him up, but if Mike went over like this he would crash down the full eight metres of the rope against the wall!

But the knot was stubborn, and struggling and pushing helplessly Mike was drawn inexorably nearer the edge.

Then he saw what had happened. On a ledge about two metres down lay the Head of Huascar, the "light" glinting like a great ruby in the red glow. It must have fallen out of Gregory's pocket somehow. Gregory, finding he couldn't reach it with one hand, had been jerking the rope lower and lower to bring him within reach. John Akobe obviously dared not pull the rope taut for fear of pulling Mike in, and was letting it out on his side as well.

"Gregory!" Mike yelled in an agony of helplessness.

"Gregory! Don't be a fool! I'll be over the edge in a minute!"

Gregory looked up, his eyes blazing. "I can't reach it!" he shrieked.

The rope jerked again, and Mike gave up trying to hold on.

Gregory touched the skull with his fingertips. Another jerk—and he knocked it off the ledge. With a scream of bafflement he hung rigid above the roaring furnace.

The skull plummeted down like a bomb, oscillating with its uneven weight. Mike could see the "light" more and more brilliant—like a falling sun—picking up the brilliance of the white heat so that he could hardly bear to look at it—until it came to rest on the thick, liquid rock three hundred metres below. It floated for a moment, in a blazing glory—then it was swallowed up for ever. . . .

13

LAST PRINCIPLES

"Good old Hyde Park!"

Mike leaned out of the taxi window.

"Never realize I'm going back to the bones and scalpels until I see Hyde Park!"

"Talking of bones," G.B. grinned; "how's the head now?"

"Considering that John Akobe had to shorten the rope and pull me off that ledge in the end—not so bad, thanks. Phew! When I think of it! If he hadn't had steel cables for muscles I'd have been smithereens now! I didn't know much about it, though—queer how shock sends you off your—oh, I'm sorry, G.B.... !"

G.B. laughed. "All right, Mike. You might say it took that to send me on to mine! I did some solid thinking in that Rio hospital; and it penetrated at last that you had more grit in your little toe than I ever had in my whole carcase!"

Mike opened his mouth, but G.B. didn't give him a chance.

"Oh, I know, I know! It was the Lord really! I know that now—but the principle's the same!" He smiled wryly. "And talking of principles, you have my full permission to flatten me if I ever call Him just a 'religious principle' again!"

Mike grinned. "Agreed! I'll smack your head for you." He leaned back and sighed contentedly—with just a speck of regret. "Oh well, it's all over now. Gregory will be busy breaking rocks for some time to come; Dan's back among his pots and manuscripts; and Keith and John Akobe have taken Huascar and the others back to Xicchu. It should all be plain sailing for them from now on, anyway."

G.B. raised a quizzical eyebrow. "Should it?"

"Well, Xicchu himself is finished, and—" Mike caught G.B.'s amused eye. "Well—fairly plain—"

"It would be, of course: once you take the Lord seriously it always is! I've noticed that!"

Mike grinned. "All right—but you know what I mean. They'll have a better chance to really build on what's been begun. They won't be bothered from that direction at least! You know, these past weeks have really convinced me of one thing. If you really want to serve Him, it doesn't matter what happens to you—He's still in control, and you're still in the palm of His hand. I don't mean He'll always get you out of things . . . !" he added hastily.

G.B. nodded. "I know what you mean."

They said nothing for a few moments. Mike gazed unseeingly at the sunny Park. He wondered what Tupac was doing. He'd liked Tupac: a lot in him. Mike was glad he'd met him. And he'd seemed as sorry as Mike had been when they'd had to split up. He'd certainly had his baptism of fire early on!

Mike chuckled suddenly.

"There's one thing certain!" he grinned. "If anybody ever tells me again that being a Christian is only for 'old ladies', I'll—I'll—"

"Smack his head?" G.B. suggested cheerfully.

"On principle!" said Mike.